Date Due

8.75

New Colleges
for
New Students

Laurence Hall
and Associates

*Foreword by Frank Newman
and Russell Edgerton*

NEW

COLLEGES

for

NEW

STUDENTS

Jossey-Bass Publishers
San Francisco · Washington · London · 1974

29056

NEW COLLEGES FOR NEW STUDENTS
by Laurence Hall and Associates

Copyright © 1974 by: Jossey-Bass, Inc., Publishers
615 Montgomery Street
San Francisco, California 94111

&

Jossey-Bass Limited
3 Henrietta Street
London WC2E 8LU

Library of Congress Catalogue Card Number LC 73-10933

International Standard Book Number ISBN 0-87589-194-2

Manufactured in the United States of America

JACKET DESIGN BY WILLI BAUM

FIRST EDITION

Code 7335

The
Jossey-Bass Series
in Higher Education

Consulting Editor

HAROLD L. HODGKINSON
University of California, Berkeley

Foreword

FRANK NEWMAN

*T*he 1950s and 1960s were exciting years in American higher education, not only for advances in scholarship but also for the progress made in the cause of social equity. Starting with passage of the GI Bill, the system was transformed by rising expectations, new forms of student aid, and a huge growth in the number and size of colleges and universities.

But, as the country has learned, opening the doors to everyone does not lead to education for everyone. This is particularly true for the new learners—the students from ghettos and farms, from all age groups and all walks of life—who do not share the social and academic orientation once taken for granted in Joe College and Betty Coed. These new learners make up fully half of the population now gaining access to higher education, but with each passing year it becomes clearer that traditional colleges are serving them poorly—and that a new diversity is needed.

There is, of course, more diversity among the institutions of higher education in the United States than we know of in any other country—schools that are two-year and four-year, public and private, religious and secular. But then no other country has ever attempted to provide a college opportunity for such a broad spectrum of its population. What is needed now is a genuinely new dimension for our diversity—schools with differing *structures of teaching and learning.* A number of innovating, nontraditional institutions have been created in recent years to meet the needs of some of our new students, but even professional educators know too little about them; our national attention remains focused on the better-known institutions.

In this book, Laurence Hall has brought together fascinating descriptive studies of sixteen of these new colleges, along with eight thought-provoking professional commentaries on the broad issues they raise. From these, the profession and the public alike can learn what is happening, what seems to work, and what can and should be done for new students.

I hope that this book serves to ignite a debate on the crucial question of how to find new and effective ways to serve these students. I also hope that it will encourage colleges and universities serving traditional students to adopt new ideas from these unusual institutions, for use in making their own programs more vital.

RUSSELL EDGERTON

The idea for this book actually occurred in government, in the summer of 1971. Congress at that time began to consider seriously a proposal for a national foundation to encourage innovation and reform throughout higher education. Since the Department of Health, Education and Welfare was to be responsible for the administration of this new agency, the HEW educational planning staff initiated several projects designed to anticipate the needs of a director and board for information about trends in higher education, what the key problems were, and what needed to be done.

Particularly lacking were studies that gave one a "feel" for the real needs and interests of the new clienteles who would be seeking more and better education in the 1970s. At the time, most people were asking, simply, how can we make colleges better? The planning staff saw the need for information concerning more fundamental issues: What are the needs and interests of the new groups of Americans now seeking postsecondary education? What educational approaches, within or without colleges, seem to be responding most successfully to these people?

With counsel from Laurence Hall of the School of Social Service Administration, University of Chicago, a project was conceived which would produce up-to-date information on "grassroots" developments taking place in behalf of learners who were presumed to have certain educational needs and interests in common. Under Hall's direction, eight experienced educational reporters were recruited and each was assigned a particular group of learners. Each reporter immersed himself in existing data about the group and then tapped various networks around the country in a search for particularly creative and responsive educational approaches. Once these were identified, the reporters visited and developed first-hand reports on a number of them.

In fashioning this book, Hall has drawn upon several of these reports, worked with the reporters in shaping them, selected education professionals for commenting on the new approaches and the learning groups they serve, and written his own summary analysis. The result is not only an unusually readable book, but one that has a multidimensional significance.

What we have, first of all, are some provocative portraits of new educational enterprises that share a common concern for the new kinds of learners seeking entry into higher education in the 1970s. This is not, by and large, an examination of institutions that have already gained visibility, but a fresh look at institutions that are usually quarantined by the operation of our present information-dissemination system.

No one should judge these particular institutions as effective simply because they were exciting enough to become magnets for an inquiring reporter. But they wouldn't have been exciting if they weren't "on to something." Indeed, they provide fascinating clues about what the educational needs and interests of various kinds of learners really are. After reading the story of the Rural Family Development project, for example, it is almost impossible to forget that in designing televised education, it is crucially important to start where the learners are. Or read about Westbrook College's marvelously personal technique for granting credit to women after they leave school, and see what happens to your enthusiasm for impersonal credit-bank arrangements.

The commentaries add another dimension by opening up

issues about the target groups themselves—including the issue of how useful it is to consider learners in terms of groups for purposes of sorting out varieties of educational approaches.

The third dimension of the book, and perhaps the most interesting of all, is the composite picture these portraits provide of the equalitarian direction in which higher education is heading. The social message of the book is that while we are still debating whether higher education should become more service-oriented and client-responsive, a number of respected and respectable educators are out there doing it. The questions this raises—about the domain of higher education, the purposes and functions of educational institutions, the appropriate standards for evaluating performance, and others—are large enough and important enough to keep us busy for some time.

It is one thing to expose equality of opportunity as a goal, but quite another to deal with the implications of that public philosophy as a reality. Practitioners looking for insights, students of education interested in educational trends and approaches, and public policy makers concerned with policies toward the emergence of new educational enterprises will all find this book provocative reading.

Frank Newman is Associate Director of University Relations, Stanford University, and chairman of the task force that wrote the 1971 "Report on Higher Education" for the Secretary of the Department of Health, Education and Welfare.

Russell Edgerton is Deputy Director, Fund for the Improvement of Postsecondary Education.

Preface

As a result of the struggle for egalitarianism in the late 1960s, many postsecondary educational institutions scurried to open their doors to students who, until then, had been largely excluded—minorities, blue-collar youth, women. Colleges proudly displayed statistics showing increased minority enrollments and pointed to new scholarship programs for the financially disadvantaged. Open-admissions policies were instituted to provide access for students with marginal secondary school records. External-degree programs, TV colleges, and correspondence schools began for those who would not or could not go to campuses. By the time President Nixon stated, in a message to Congress in 1971, that "no student who wants to attend college should be prevented from doing so," he was articulating for federal policy a goal already embraced by much of the postsecondary education community.

By the end of the 1960s, however, it was evident that access, by itself, is not enough. Pressure for additional reform was mounting steadily. From almost every direction came recommendations for reform—from individuals, public and private commissions, governmental studies, and reports of higher-education associations. It was the era of commissions: the Scranton Commission, the Assembly on Goals and Governance, the Newman Report, the Carnegie Commission on Higher Education, the Commission on Non-Traditional

Study. Their findings included some alarming statistics about the failure of the system to engage and hold its students. According to Newman's *Report on Higher Education* (issued by the Department of Health, Education and Welfare in the spring of 1971), "Only about one third [of those who enter college each year] will ever complete a four-year course of study." The dropout rate for the "new student" was even more alarming. For example, Martin Mayer, writing in the February 1972 issue of *Commentary* magazine about the open-admissions program in New York City, reported that "half of those who did enter left during the first two years." Clearly, if the postsecondary education community is going to carry the egalitarian commitment beyond its doorstep, it must provide a more rewarding educational experience for the new students.

The colleges described in this book can play an important role in the search for effective education for the new students. Unlike many colleges today that are expanding their potential student clientele (for example, Catholic men's schools that are becoming more secular and going coeducational), these colleges are willing to stake their future on meeting the needs of a very specialized student clientele. This can be a risky venture, particularly when the college focuses on the "high-risk" student. However, it opens the opportunity to test new solutions that, if found successful, may be implemented in other settings. In this way, these colleges can be seen as not only important in their own right but as laboratories for the discovery and examination of the needs of new students and as testing grounds for examination of long-standing assumptions about education.

The format of the book is intended to stimulate an exchange of ideas about the educational needs of the new students and how best to meet these needs. Descriptive studies of colleges that have been designed to serve particular groups of new students are followed by commentaries written by educators who have thought seriously about the educational needs of those students. These commentators were given broad latitude in preparing their contributions, and were encouraged to use the reports on particular colleges only as springboards for their own thinking.

In reading this book, be assured that we are aware of its limitations. The student groups selected as the focus of the book are not the only new students. The schools described are not meant to represent the full range of institutions and programs that have been developed in response to the new students. In fact, since the descriptive studies are based on information gathered in the fall of 1971 for a report commissioned by the Department of Health, Education and Welfare, they should be seen as characterizing only the nature of innovative activity at that particular time. And the views of the commentators are not the only observations that could be offered. Our purpose has been not to write a definitive statement on what is happening in postsecondary education in response to the new students, but rather to stimulate further debate. We believe that this book raises many more questions than it answers, and we hope that the reader will choose to become a participant in the continuing discussion of how postsecondary education can be made more responsive to the needs of the new students.

The staff of the project thank those who have assisted in this survey. Russell Edgerton, Deputy Director of the Fund for the Improvement of Postsecondary Education, was a key partner in the original design of the project and provided ongoing consultation. Other members of the HEW planning staff, such as Martin Kramer and Bernie Martin, provided valuable consultation at crucial junctures. Don Stewart, assistant to the president at the University of Pennsylvania, and Cyril Houle, professor of education at the University of Chicago, provided important consultation on the final report. Nancy Ward provided the secretarial support necessary to meet the many deadlines and to unravel the complicated traveling schedules at HEW, and Betsy Fimoff was responsible for all of the secretarial support that moved this from a project manuscript to book form. These people should share any success the book enjoys, and be held blameless for any of its shortcomings.

Chicago   LAURENCE HALL
September 1973

Contents

Contributors

PETER H. BINZEN is Urban Affairs Editor of the
Philadelphia Bulletin. He is the author of
Whitetown USA and the co-author of
The Wreck of the Penn Central.

ELIAS BLAKE, JR., is President of the Institute for Services
to Education in Washington, D.C., a non-profit corporation
specializing in the problems of greater access to higher
education for blacks.

PASTORA SAN JUAN CAFFERTY is Assistant Professor,
School of Social Service Adminstration,
University of Chicago, where she is chairman of the
University of Chicago Faculty Study Committee
on Ethnicity.

K. PATRICIA CROSS holds a joint appointment as
Senior Research Psychologist at the Educational Testing
Service and Research Educator at the Center for
Higher Education, University of California, Berkeley.
She is the author of *Beyond the Open Door*.

MARGARET C. DUNKLE is currently Project Associate with the Project on the Status and Education of Women at the Association of American Colleges.

JOHN EGERTON is a freelance journalist in Nashville, Tennessee. He is the author of *State Universities and Black Americans* and *The Public Black College: Integration and Disintegration.*

LAURENCE HALL is Associate Dean, The School of Social Service Administration, The University of Chicago.

ELISABETH HANSOT is in the Office of Planning and Management, National Institute of Education, Department of Health, Education and Welfare.

HAROLD L. HODGKINSON is Research Educator at the Center for Research and Development in Higher Education, University of California, Berkeley. He is the co-author of *Power and Authority* and *Identity Crisis in Higher Education.*

CYRIL O. HOULE is Professor of Education, University of Chicago, and author of *The Design of Education* and *The External Degree.*

PETER A. JANSSEN is Education Editor of *Saturday Review/World.* He has also written for *Newsweek,* the *Philadelphia Inquirer, Washingtonian,* and *American Education.*

JOSEPH MICHALAK is Editor of *Day Care and Early Education.* He was previously Editor of *Education News* and Associate Education Editor of *The New York Herald Tribune.*

PATRICIA LOCKE is Director, Planning Resources in
Minority Education, Western Interstate Commission for
Higher Education.

LARRY VAN DYNE is a former education reporter for
the *Boston Globe* and is presently reporting for the
Chronicle of Higher Education.

New Colleges
for
New Students

⁊ 1 ⸎

Blue-Collar and
Rural Youth

*M*ost high school graduates now
enter college. For the first time in history, it is the common rather
than the uncommon thing to do. As a 1972 study by the American
Council on Education (*The American Freshman: National Norms
for Fall 1972*) shows, the majority of college freshmen in the 1970s
are the sons and daughters of parents who have had no college
experience; they are first-generation college students. Never before,
and probably never again, will we have such a large education gap
between parents and their children.

Parents whose children are venturing into a world unknown
to them frequently express mingled feelings of pride, concern, and
suspicion. Young people are leaving the familiarity of the accepted
customs and values of the home to be exposed to new ideas, broader
perspectives, and a wider diversity of people. They face insecurity,
the challenge of new experiences, and divided loyalties between the
old and the new.

Some colleges, often those in isolated geographical regions,
have had long years of experience in cushioning the cultural shock

to acceptable proportions for both students and parents. Alice Lloyd College, deep in the mountains of Kentucky, is one such college. Since 1923 it has been preparing rural Appalachian youth for their more cosmopolitan futures. At the other end of the spectrum is the brand-new Fiorello H. La Guardia Community College, located just across the East River from midtown Manhattan. Its mission is to serve an urban industrialized population of recent emigrants from Italy, Ireland, Germany, and Greece. The work of these two colleges is described in this chapter.

🎵 La Guardia Community College 🎵

Peter H. Binzen

In the fall of 1970 New York City's Board of Higher Education put into effect an open-admissions policy, guaranteeing places in the City University of New York (CUNY) for all interested city high school graduates regardless of their academic records. Those in the top half of their high school graduating classes or with averages of eighty and above were to be taken into the senior four-year colleges. All others were to be accommodated at CUNY's expanding two-year community colleges. One of these colleges, Fiorello H. La Guardia Community College, in the Long Island City section of Queens, opened a year later to help handle the crush of students that took advantage of CUNY's open door.

Long Island City, listed as one of New York's eleven poverty areas, is a blue-collar district just across the East River from midtown Manhattan. Its median family income of just over $6000 is lower than that in Queens generally and in the city as a whole. Its unemployment rate is higher than in the rest of the borough and city. It is heavily industrialized. Big trucks rumble along its main arteries day and night, and air pollution is a critical problem. Though much of its housing is adequate, there are increasing signs of deterioration. About 80 percent of its population is white, largely of Italian, Irish, German, and Greek extraction; and most of its

Editor's Note: The descriptive studies of new colleges are based on information gathered in the fall of 1971 for a report commissioned by the Department of Health, Education and Welfare.

families have been in this country for no more than 'one or two generations. The area is 70 percent Roman Catholic and 65 percent Democratic. However, it produced more than normal turnouts for Barry Goldwater in 1964 and for James L. Buckley, the victorious Conservative Party candidate for senator in 1970.

According to the 1960 census, Long Island City's adults over the age of twenty-five averaged between nine and ten years of schooling (below the city-wide average)'. Its two academic high schools ranked among the six lowest on reading scores out of sixteen schools in Queens. The proportion of students from these two schools applying for college was substantially below that in the borough and city. Queens, meanwhile, was New York City's fastest-growing borough in the 1960s but had the lowest number of community college places in the fall of 1967.

It was clear to CUNY's planners that Long Island City needed a community college, but they were not sure that it wanted one. The young people there surpassed their parents' level of formal education just by completing high school. "Since many of them come from low-income families," a CUNY study explained, "the short-term gain of 'money in my pocket' through employment immediately after high school cannot fail to be attractive. Consequently, it appears that an intensive information and recruiting program will be needed to get many of these students to apply to colleges." The study also found that "many of the adults tend to be rigid in their thinking," and that only a "big selling job" would get them to accept the idea of having a college student in the family.

So Fiorello H. La Guardia Community College had to tailor its appeal to Long Island City's skeptical ethnic whites. To do so, the planners decided that the college would operate out of a converted factory once used by Sperry Rand and surrounded by other factories and light industry. More important, its students would not just go to classes; they would also go to work. CUNY's top administration recommended that La Guardia try some kind of work-study program. Joseph Shenker, the thirty-one-year-old president, and his staff went one better than that. They decided to try something that, to their knowledge, had never been tried before: an "all co-op" community college.

Cooperative education at the college level is about sixty-five years old, but the usual practice is to limit the co-op program to one department or division of a college or university. For example, at the University of Cincinnati, where it all started, or at Drexel University in Philadelphia, a relatively small proportion of the total enrollment enters the cooperative program.

At La Guardia Community College the decision was made to require all students to participate. All would work at full-time outside jobs for three of their eight quarters at La Guardia. For this work they would receive nine credits toward the sixty-seven they needed to graduate, and the jobs were expected to pay about two dollars an hour. Shenker and his staff believed that the educational advantages would be at least as important as the plan's economic advantages to the students. They were determined to integrate off-campus and on-campus learning.

In the fall of 1970 La Guardia administrators began an intensive campaign to recruit students for the first entering class. They mailed letters to 18,000 students in Queens high schools, urging them to consider La Guardia and to "start a chain reaction of awareness about this new and different work-study college." They held community meetings to break down the resistance of parents. They consulted church leaders. The results of this largest recruitment campaign in CUNY's history were heartening. Fourteen hundred New York high school seniors picked La Guardia as their first or second choice, and about 575 were chosen for the freshman class. "There's no doubt in my mind that parents in this community like this kind of college," said Sheila Gordon, associate dean of cooperative education. "They're ecstatic about the idea of kids making money while working for degrees. The kids are excited, too, some because they need to make money and others because they don't know what they want to do and welcome a chance to sample jobs."

Long before the start of school, La Guardia administrators set to work to "humanize the education process." After its first class had been selected, La Guardia staff members went to the sending high schools and spoke individually to about 80 percent of the incoming freshmen. They invited students to the college for a day. While workmen painted walls and nailed partitions in the reconverted factory, the newcomers met with La Guardia faculty members and student leaders from other CUNY colleges. Each student met with a counselor or faculty member and designed his or her own program. The meetings were by appointment and there were no lines. After registration, William Stevenson, then associate dean of students, scheduled a one-day workshop to set up various task forces—student activities, academic affairs, publications, athletics, governance, drugs—that would work in the summer. Eighty-seven students, nearly one fourth of the enrollment, showed up. Finally, the week before classes began, fifty students attended a two-day "student leader institute," which prepared them to conduct a two-day orientation for the rest of the class. Eighty percent of the students showed up for the voluntary orientation, and the high percentage was strong testimony to the enthusiasm and hope that careful plans had elicited. As one administrator said, "The whole concept of a school's being warm and human was new to the students."

Unlike all other units within CUNY, La Guardia runs on a twelve-month basis. Students get one week off at the end of each quarter, but there is no summer vacation. All students are required to take at least one course in each of four divisions—business, language and culture, personality and society, the natural environment. First-year students take courses during the first two quarters. In the second year they alternate jobs and course work, each taking two of the four quarters, so that half the class is in school and half out on jobs at all times. (About half of La Guardia's students have part-time jobs of their own that are unrelated to the cooperative program.) La Guardia intends to match students with work in their areas of interests. Women students taking the secretarial science course are to get secretarial jobs. Those studying business, accounting, retail management, and data processing are lined up with positions in those fields. Liberal-arts transfer students who are uncertain of their job interests sample in various areas.

When I visited La Guardia at its opening in September 1971, the first work experiences were still six months away. Eight full-time staffers were seeking internships among sixty to seventy employers, including banks, stores, factories, and public agencies; and joint appointments had been made in La Guardia's co-op and business departments. Four hundred freshmen were placed in jobs in the spring and summer of 1972. In the fall that followed, there was some student attrition, but about one hundred and eighty were placed in jobs by eighty employers. Meanwhile, nine-hundred first-year students were admitted in September 1972, raising the total enrollment to thirteen hundred.

The true test of cooperative education comes when the students attempt to integrate what they learn on their jobs with what they are learning in the classroom. "Co-op is not something that can be hooked onto the academic program," one administrator said. "Teaching here may be difficult. The faculty will face challenges from students who may say, 'Look, what you just told us isn't what I learned outside.'" Recognizing that its central challenge is directly to link what students learn on the outside with what goes on in the classroom, the administration at La Guardia plans a series of tie-ins. Co-op advisors will visit all the interns at least once at their place of employment. Every week interns will return to the college for meetings with co-op staffers and faculty members. Faculty members themselves have been directed to adapt their courses to the outside work experiences.

La Guardia is trying hard to succeed with its cooperative education program. Dr. Shenker, a young, low-key president, sees the college's goals as crucially important. "It's a tough nut to crack," he said of co-op education. "Nobody in the country is doing it well. I don't know if we can pull it off. If we do, I'll be very pleased."

Alice Lloyd College

Larry Van Dyne

The college's dining hall hangs from the side of a steep, tree-covered mountain, its backside flush against the hill and its front porch jutting into midair atop a row of stone pillars. The faculty members and students who have answered the college's rusty dinner bell move off the porch through the front door; the noon meal is about to begin. A small chime signals a hush over the dining room, and an elderly science professor offers a short blessing.

Each table is set for eight, and people quickly scoot the wicker benches up to the tables and begin passing the food—

country food: mashed potatoes, sliced tomatoes, green beans, pork chops, biscuits, and milk. The room is poorly lit—the central fixture is a wagon-wheel chandelier with sixty-watt bulbs. The roof is held up by tree poles taken directly from the woods, and the wooden floor sags in places, its boards showing fifty years of wear.

Fall 1971. Pippa Passes, Kentucky. It is noon at Alice Lloyd College, deep in the mountains of southeastern Kentucky, in the heart of coal country, just a few miles from where the Hatfields and McCoys used to fight it out. A two-year college with fewer than three hundred students, Alice Lloyd is perhaps the most remarkable of a group of colleges that have as their clientele the mountain youths of Appalachia. During the last two decades this region, whose very name has historically stood for poverty and isolation, has been in the midst of an unsettling era of outmigration and change. And in this secluded little valley, nearly 150 miles from the bluegrass country around Lexington, Alice Lloyd College has built an impressive record of preparing Appalachian students for a more cosmopolitan future. More later on how it does that. The first thing one has to know about this college is its fascinating past, a past that is well symbolized by the warm, down-home quality of the old dining hall (which is scheduled to be replaced soon). That past is intimately tied up with the life of Alice Lloyd herself. (Mrs. Lloyd died in 1962 at the age of eighty-seven, and the college's name was changed then in her memory.)

The daughter of a comfortable Back Bay Boston family, Mrs. Lloyd spent three years at Radcliffe in the early 1900s before her father died and she was forced to leave school and support her mother as a journalist and chautauqua lecturer. A few years later Mrs. Lloyd herself was struck by a case of spinal meningitis that left her right arm permanently paralyzed. Doctors advised her to seek a better climate outside New England.

Friends suggested that she move to the mountains of eastern Kentucky and claim a cottage that had been abandoned there by an abortive Presbyterian mission. Mrs. Lloyd accepted the advice, and after a long buggy ride from Boston she and her mother arrived in 1915. They found the cottage's roof caving in and its floor beginning to rot, but even at that their new home was much better than the other homes in the area. Mrs. Lloyd was horrified by the

poverty she found around her and mystified by the hostility the
natives displayed toward people from outside the mountains. She
began trying to break down their suspicion by teaching their children in her old cottage.

Before the first year passed, a farmer named Bysh Johnson
arrived at Mrs. Lloyd's door and offered her fifty acres of land and
a new cottage if she would move a few miles into another valley
and teach his nine children. She agreed and in the spring of 1916
moved into the new house that Johnson had built for her on the
bank of Caney Creek. The site, where the college now stands, was a
typical eastern Kentucky valley or "hollow." The quiet-flowing little
creek was flanked on each side by narrow strips of flat-bottom land
cut short by the steep rise of the tree-covered mountains. Today the
college's wooden and stone buildings fill up those flat spaces along
the sides of the creek, which is spanned by footbridges. On one side
a winding road takes up much of the available space, so that the
college has been forced to stack the dining hall, the Pippa Passes
rural post office, and several faculty houses like stairsteps up the
side of the mountain.

When Mrs. Lloyd started teaching at Caney Creek, more
than 250 years after the New England Puritans founded Harvard,
eastern Kentucky still had only a few elementary schools. They
usually offered only six grades, and there were no high schools
worth mentioning. Only two of every hundred of the county's citizens had been to high school. Mrs. Lloyd, seeking volunteers to
spend a few weeks or months teaching the children of the illiterate
mountaineers, began writing friends in the North. As a result of her
efforts, scores of volunteers, often Radcliffe or Wellesley friends,
poured into the region to teach. If they could not come themselves,
they often sent money or books. Within ten years Mrs. Lloyd is
believed to have started perhaps one thousand elementary schools
and at least fifteen high schools in this part of the state. One of the
high schools still sits near the college, and all have now been turned
into public schools.

Mrs. Lloyd was convinced that if eastern Kentucky was ever
to pull out of its misery and backwardness, it required indigenous
leadership. This meant educating the young mountaineers beyond
high school. She therefore added courses to one of her high schools

and in 1923 graduated seven students from an unaccredited institution called Caney Junior College. With donations, she sent them on to four-year schools. Five of them eventually became doctors and two became schoolteachers. On a shoestring budget she ran the college like this for nearly forty years, producing dozens of other leaders for the mountains.

The college that Mrs. Lloyd founded is now fully accredited and enrolls about 285 students. Ninety percent are natives of the small towns and hollows of the twenty-two mountain counties of eastern Kentucky; nearly all are fresh out of high school. Fifty percent are the first of their immediate families to go to college, and 30 percent are the first to make it through high school. Their average family income is $3000 a year, and virtually all work to pay their way through school. Although the college's official tuition is $1600 a year, use of federal subsidies and private scholarships has reduced the average out-of-pocket payment for students to about $300.

Because of its geographic inaccessibility and its introverted culture, this region where most Alice Lloyd students come from has been considered one of the most isolated sections of the nation, a world typified in many people's minds by stout whiskey, bloody feuds, and dusty coal mines. Throughout the 1960s, however, Appalachia started to open up. When the local coal industry automated, many natives went north to find work and returned on weekends and holidays, bringing back influences from outside the region. The highways built by the Appalachian Regional Commission and the presence of television have opened further the once closed mountain society.

These influences mean that Alice Lloyd's students are not as isolated from mainstream America as they once were. One sees here the bell-bottoms and long hair of the contemporary national student culture, for instance. But for many of the college's students, the urban and suburban world that most American youths take for granted is at times confusing and frightening. Members of the college choir, for instance, are sometimes reluctant to try new, unfamiliar food when they are touring outside their native region. One student, who had never traveled in the Deep South, admits that he was fooled on one choir tour when he was served grits. "I thought it was cream of wheat, so I took a whole bowlful," he says. "I really didn't like it, but I ate it all anyway."

Some Alice Lloyd students also are emotionally dependent on their families in a way that makes it difficult for them to break their ties with home. As a result of generations of intermarriage, they have kin scattered throughout the mountains. There are Slones, Halls, Combs, Caudills, and Allens in hollow after hollow for miles around. Nearly a third of the 150 entries in the Pippa Passes phone book are Slones. Homesickness strikes students fairly regularly, even though they may be only twenty miles from where they were born and raised; more than one homesick student has been coaxed back to the campus by concerned faculty members. Although 80 percent of the students live on campus, the dormitories are virtually deserted on weekends.

The high school experiences of Alice Lloyd students—often in a school of fewer than one hundred students or in a somewhat larger, recently consolidated county-seat school—have left many of them without the skills needed for conventional college study: reading comprehension, vocabulary, clarity in speech and writing. On national tests of these skills, they usually score about the twenty-fifth percentile (average for students in that part of the country). Many are impatient with books and have difficulty concentrating on a printed page for more than a few minutes. If they do acquire an interest in book learning, they are bucking an anti-intellectual tradition that runs deep here and threatens them with social ostracism. It is difficult to break away from two staples of contemporary Appalachian culture, cars and basketball. Says a faculty member, who is disappointed that no one seems to be using the college library: "If we could just turn the energy they devote to basketball into an English class we'd have a winner for sure." There also is little support for education from home. One example: A homesick girl, who had called her mother to come get her, was almost persuaded by a faculty member to stay in school. But the mother leaned out the car window to have the final word. "You mean to tell me," she said scoldingly, "that I drove all the way over here for nothing."

In 1962, when Mrs. Lloyd died, the presidency of the college was assumed by William Hayes, a dean who already had been gradually assuming the leadership of the college in Mrs. Lloyd's last years. A soft-spoken Missourian then in his early forties, Hayes had been with the college since 1942, when he got his master's degree at the University of Missouri and then answered one of Mrs. Lloyd's recruiting letters. He had left only once, to study at the University of Wisconsin during the late stages of World War II, but had been drawn back to Kentucky. Hayes understood and respected the mountaineers, and he appreciated the struggle of Mrs. Lloyd to set up the college. But he sensed that Appalachia was changing—becoming more open—and that the college also had to change if it was to retain its educational leadership role.

In Mrs. Lloyd's day the college had discovered talented youths, encouraged and protected them, sent them out to get more education, and expected them to come back to lead their people out of poverty. But by the 1960s outmigrations, television, new roads, and other influences started to open up the region; public colleges were beginning to compete for Alice Lloyd's clientele; and more of its students were coming from small towns than from the deeply isolated hollows. Hayes felt that the time had arrived for the college to develop more contacts with the outside world and to force its students into situations where they would have to do the same. "We made up our minds," he says, "that we had to challenge our students with things that they were not good at and that we as a college weren't good at." One can find this policy of outreach all over the campus now, in its buildings, its people, and its program. Just a few examples:

Near the old wooden dining hall stands a modern science building, opened in 1970 after years of careful planning by the staff with the advice of leading science educators. Its flexible design encourages close contact between faculty and students, facilitates individualized instruction, and avoids obsolescence in ways that make it a model for college science facilities around the country. According to Hayes, this building, rather than the dining hall, is now the symbol of the college.

The college has created a "board of educational advisors," which includes big-name higher-education specialists from every corner of the country, to react to its plans for new programs or curricular changes. "We developed that board with two purposes in mind—what we needed to learn from the rest of the nation and what the rest of the nation needed to learn about us," says Hayes. "It was darned difficult three or four years ago for educators to think that such a small and remote college could be so far ahead in its thinking. This board gave us currency and acceptability."

Hayes has established personal contacts with people in the higher-education field across the country; he keeps up with the latest educational literature; and he is an influential member of the American Association of Community and Junior Colleges. He was entrusted recently with the chairmanship of the association's federal relations committee. (It didn't hurt any that Representative Carl Perkins, who is quite influential on federal education legislation, once went to Alice Lloyd and represented this district.)

The college has begun raising the percentage of its students from outside the region and eventually hopes to reach 20 percent— enough, Hayes thinks, to bring in new ideas and points of view. Already one of the outsiders has started a campus craze for a new game—called ping-pong. Several Alice Lloyd students now take part in two- to four-week exchanges with colleges in Massachusetts, Ohio, Wisconsin, California, Tennessee, and Illinois. Others take co-op jobs in other states, and there are other contacts through the tours of the Voices of Appalachia choir.

In 1965 the college started an experiential education program called ALCOR (Alice Lloyd College Outreach), in which students perform health, education, and community-development work in the poorest hollows throughout the mountains. ALCOR does not take students outside of Appalachia (some work in hollows where they or their families are well known, in fact), but the experience is often as broadening and eye-opening as the trips outside the mountains. From it, one senses, many students develop the notion that their lives can have an impact on others, and they begin to develop the commitment to service that Mrs. Lloyd stressed among her first students.

These attempts to break the college and its students out of Appalachian isolation are important; but to the outsider who has grown weary of the slick, hyped-up "innovation" of so many colleges other aspects of the Alice Lloyd experience seem worth looking at more closely. There is something about the atmosphere of the place, something about the style of the faculty and staff, something about the way they go about their everyday teaching that seems just right—and important—for these students. One gets some sense of it from peeking in on a class in Appalachian sociology and taking a look at the Appalachian Oral History Project, which goes a long way in helping students take pride in their own roots.

Laurence Baldridge's class in Sociology of the Southern Highlands is meeting an hour early, 8:30 instead of 9:30. That will give him time to load his students aboard the college's old school bus and make the drive along the winding blacktop to Hindman, fifteen miles to the west. He has arranged for the class to attend a trial being held there at the Knott County courthouse. The defendant is Bill Cohen, a former Alice Lloyd professor, who is charged with obstructing a state highway in October 1970, when he attempted to block a line of coal trucks leaving a strip mine.

Cohen is one of the more flamboyant of a small cadre of environmentalists who are fighting the strip mines, the coal-extraction technique that is systematically decapitating the mountains around here and causing a major environmental disaster. The huge trucks that carry the coal from the mines are usually wider and heavier than the laws allows—or so the environmentalists say—and have caused several accidents as well as turning the highways in places into a nearly impassable jumble of chuckholes. Cohen, it seems, decided to dramatize the situation by sitting in front of a coal truck that was coming down from a mountain strip mine and preparing to enter a state highway. A huge American flag in one hand and a white Bible in the other, he stood in front of a line of trucks for nearly forty-five minutes until he was arrested by state police.

Baldridge's bus rolls up in front of the two-story stone courthouse. Before he lets the students out and goes down the street to park, he pauses to offer them some guidance about things to look for and think about: "See if you think he gets as fair a trial with a name like Cohen as he would if it were Combs," he says. Inside, the big second-floor courtroom is empty except for thirty or so elderly jurors, who are waiting to see if they will be called in this case. The men are on the right side of the room, the women are on the left. In the spectator section, directly in front of the bench, are a few of Cohen's supporters. As soon as the students arrive, a well-dressed, middle-age woman begins circulating among them a petition that asks the legislature to ban strip mining from the state. Alice Slone, one of Alice Lloyd's early protégées who now runs a nearby school and fights the mines, is there. So is Jack Weller, a minister whose participant-observer study of the mountaineers, *Yesterday's People,* is one of the books Baldridge's students are reading. Weller promises he will come to class the following week to talk about the book.

The process of impaneling a jury takes perhaps thirty minutes. Cohen's lawyer, Dan Martin, himself one of the first graduates of Caney Junior College, questions prospective jurors about their connections to the strip-mine industry. With years of experience in these parts, Martin is aware of the central problem of the antimining environmentalists—that mountain folk are reluctant to join any antimining movement because so many are dependent on the mines for jobs. He also displays an amazing grasp of local family trees. Those people he doesn't know he asks, "Now who was your daddy?" or "Doesn't your brother drive a coal truck?" If the answers reveal a connection to the mines, he asks that the juror be dismissed.

The prosecution calls its first witness, the state policeman who arrested Cohen. He says that Cohen was arrested because he was out on the highway blocking a lane of traffic. The reason, Cohen says, was that the trucks pushed him there. In his turn, Martin forces the trooper to admit that he did not bother to check the width and weight of the coal trucks that were the source of the controversy. "You mean to tell me," says Martin, pushing the point further, "that you arrested this man in this confrontation and you didn't even bother to get the names of the truck drivers?" The trooper says he could only do so many things at once. Another trooper tells essentially the same story, the jury breaks to eat, and the class has to get back to the college. Everyone will have to wait until the next morning to learn from the *Louisville Courier Journal* that Cohen was convicted and fined $100 but that he refused to pay the fine and spent the night in the county jail.

Out of jail, Cohen comes to the sociology class a couple of days later to discuss the trial and the anti-mining movement. From their questions, it is clear that the students have not been greatly impressed by the justice of the Kentucky judicial system. They speculate on the motives behind the judge's procedural rulings, on why the jury was composed totally of old people, on whether the police and courts are owned by the coal industry, and whether they themselves—since many of them have relatives driving coal trucks—could have been fair in judging the evidence. Baldridge, who has an unusual background as a mountain preacher with a master's degree in urban sociology, patiently interjects only an occasional guiding question or comment and allows students and Cohen to carry the bulk of the discussion.

At the end of the class, he gives students the schedule for the rest of the week. The following day a candidate for governor who is making a campaign swing through the country will be in class. He will be followed by a poverty lawyer, then a regional planner. The students also will hear a tape made by some members of the class when they drove to Whitesburg to interview Harry Caudill, the lawyer and author of *Night Comes to the Cumberlands,* which is the best available book on Appalachia and one they have been assigned. Baldridge also checks on the progress of their written reports—reports on schools, strip mining, local politics, roads, unions, feuds, and so on.

Not all classes at Alice Lloyd make such frequent use of field trips and outside speakers at this. The lecture method has not been entirely abandoned here. But because classes are small, because students have special learning problems, and because they are excited by concrete rather than abstract kinds of learning, classes are rare that depend totally on lectures as a teaching technique. One often finds scenes like these, which are too rare in many colleges: Two barefoot girls, one with a stopwatch dangling from her neck and the other with a ten-foot metal tape measure, are wading in Caney Creek. For a geology class, they are determining how long it takes a chip of styrofoam to float ten feet, so that they can estimate the velocity of the water and make judgments about erosion. . . . A heavy-set freshman girl is puffing up a road along the side of the mountain; she is being timed so that students can measure her horsepower for a physics class. . . . An Upward Bound student is out in the creek building a pollution-control device from an old basket and screen wire.

On the south side of the creek, students drift into Bill Weinberg's office nearly all hours of the day to pick up or return tape recorders, to get fresh cassettes, or to transcribe interviews. They are involved in the Appalachian Oral History Project, which was started in the summer of 1971 under a small grant from the National Endowment for the Humanities. Weinberg—a young lawyer from Virginia, a former poverty worker, and son-in-law of a former Kentucky governor—is director of the project.

The students, from Alice Lloyd and nearby Lees Junior College, track down and interview old-timers in the six counties around their campuses. Before these people die, the students are trying to continue on tape some of the rich regional history that has been passed down by word of mouth but has never, in this land of high illiteracy, been written down. They have conducted more than two hundred hours of interviews with retired miners, teachers, storekeepers, loggers, postmasters, lawyers, moonshiners, and preachers. Questioning in a mountain dialect that establishes easy rapport with their subjects, the students have drawn out colorful and valuable stories of feuds, coal towns, railroads, floods, union organizing, superstitions, religion, folk cures, politics, race relations, schools, farming, and logging; they have even managed to record several songs sung by these old Appalachians. Just to give a flavor of the interviews, here is one with Thomas (Buddy) Hall, an eighty-seven-year-old retired Pike County storekeeper-postmaster-moonshiner, who tells about Bad Talt (rhymes with stout) Hall, one of the fiercest bad men in a region that has produced more than its share:

Student: *Who was it killed Bad Talt—or do you know?*

Hall: *He hung. They hung him out at Wise [Virginia]. Ya see he was own-born cousin to my daddy. Own-born cousin, Bad Talt was.*

Student: *How many people did he kill?*

Hall: *Twenty-two.*

Student: *What did he kill them for? Just mean or what?*

Hall: *Aw mean! He wasn't mean when he growed up. First*

time he ever shot anybody come up over election. Come up over the old man Captain Bowling and one of the Tripletts runnin' fer assessor way back in the ole days. Talt married in to one of these Tripletts and one of these Triplett men wanted Talt to be fer his man. Talt told him no, said I got to vote for Old Man Captain, says on account of he's my uncle. He went in and voted and when he come back out this here Triplett jumped and kicked his hind end. Talt run off and took to the woods. He run off and was gone about an hour and when he come back he come back with a pistol and he killed one of 'em.

Student: *How old was he when he killed his first man?*

Hall: *Talt was round up in twenty just a little, maybe not much up in twenty.*

Student: *How old did he live to be?*

Hall: *Aw, he was hung at up in thirty.*

"These kids have heard a lot of these stories before from their grandma or grandpa," says Weinberg, "but they were inclined to dismiss them as just the old folks talking." (The interviewer above is a grandnephew of the subject.) Weinberg says the fact that students are paid work-study money to take such tales down and that actors, novelists, and historians come round to study them heightens their appreciation of their subculture. The work also helps, he says, to develop their ability to talk to other people, to overcome the shyness that is one of their most common traits. Here is what Kenny Slone, an Alice Lloyd freshman who worked on the project in the summer between high school and college, wrote about his experience:

> *There are certain things that I have always wanted to know about eastern Kentucky. Feuds have always fascinated me; old tales and superstitions have always led me on. Most of all I have always wanted to know something about my family tree.*
> *We tried to take people from all sides, big shots such*

*as Ruby Watts, Merd Slone, Sheldon Maggard, B. F. Reed,
and others. While we also took little shots such as Jake
Fraley, Shellie Smith, Mr. Foster, Mrs. Will Thacker, and
others. We put these together and find out their differences.
To see how their young life were much the same but their
older lives are so different. Why the big shots made something of their self, while the little shots didn't. The reason
was mainly . . . education.*

*We have two stories on our Congressman, Carl D.
Perkins. We have a big buildup from his sister Bevie Pratt.
We also have his letdown from Canton Reynolds.*

*At the answer of our first question we get a quivering
voice. Then we get into the childhood and the voice length-
ening out, a distant stare comes across his face as he recol-
lects his younger childhood. Suddenly, before he realizes it
we have his entire life on tape. Maybe not his entire life but
enough to show us what he did and how he lived.*

*So the interview is completed and we now have in-
formation we did not have before. We have questions that
we can ask on our next interview. The best thing of all is
that we have this old man's voice on tape, and after he is
dead we can still hear him talk. The old man or woman's
great-grandchildren can hear him talk even after they are
gone.*

Some of the people we interviewed were:

*—Emma Foster, a kindly old woman who lives in
Drift, Kentucky. Her husband was a coal miner for many
years. She did not tell us very much because in my opinion
she acted as if she wanted to forget the hard past.*

*—Jake Fraley, a retired miner who also lives in
Drift, Kentucky. He has worked hard all of his life and he
told us about his dreaded past as a teenager growing up in a
mining camp.*

*—B. F. Reed. We get a different story from him be-
cause he was the owner of the Elkhorn mine that a lot of
miners worked for back then. He looks is if he never did do
a hard day's work in his life.*

I have gained much knowledge of the country, the

*knowledge of the past, old tales, superstitious tales, and most
of all I have found out something about my family tree from
the Slones we have interviewed. This program has been a
big benefit to me. Why? When I came here I really didn't
expect to go back to college anywhere. But I became interested in this program and decided to work here if possible,
so here I am and I think I will like going back to school.*

*I have something else I have been trying to gain for
years and have failed. That is the best thing this program
has done for me. It has gave me confidence in myself as a
talker. I am proud that I have worked on Oral History. I
don't expect to ever make any speeches but I am no longer
afraid to go up to someone and start talking to them like I
have known them for years.*

Hearing this testimony one begins to appreciate the drastic
human impact of the climate, the people, and the programs that
are blended here in this little college tucked away in the mountains.
One begins to understand that it has come up with just the right
combination of support and challenge for its mountain students.

Commentary: Meeting the Needs of Blue-Collar and Rural Youth

K. Patricia Cross

Fiorello H. La Guardia Community College and Alice Lloyd
College present some vivid contrasts. One was founded a half century before the nation built up substantial pressure for college for
lower-class youth; the other was founded in 1971, at the height of
national awareness of inequality of educational opportunity. One
college is located in urban, industrialized New York City; the other,
in rural, isolated Pippa Passes, Kentucky. Alice Lloyd serves the
children of people whose families have lived in the hills of Kentucky
for generations; La Guardia serves the children of recent emigrants
from Europe. Alice Lloyd is a residential campus; La Guardia is a
commuter campus. And yet, as different as these two colleges at first
seem, their student populations have much in common. Their
parents are poorly educated and poorly paid, and they live in sub-

standard housing. Politically, they are conservative, and their lives
are circumscribed by religious and cultural tradition. The task of the
colleges is to build a sturdy bridge between the past and the futures
of these first-generation college students.

Although two-year colleges in rural and blue-collar America
do not often make the lists of innovative and experimental colleges,
such colleges exist on the cutting edge of change. They open upon a
new era of egalitarian postsecondary education, and they symbolize
the commitment of a nation to equality of educational opportunity.
Traditional higher education has had little experience with the
kinds of students who attend Alice Lloyd and La Guardia. But we
are beginning to learn something about what lies ahead if we are
to provide for the educational needs of these students. Research
provides us with a statistical description of the characteristics of
these young people as a group. Experience, experimentation, and
evaluation will help us to devise appropriate learning experiences.

Nationally, the largest number of students walking through
the open doors of colleges today are poor students—academically as
well as financially.[1] They do not enter college because they have
enjoyed school in the past or because they expect to enjoy their college study. As a matter of fact, they are more likely than traditional
college students to say that the classroom makes them nervous. What
they hope to get out of college is the passport to a good job and some
of the material benefits that traditional college students are re-
nouncing.

Some of the attitudes that traditional students have most
vociferously disavowed are held by substantial numbers of the new
students. Examples: "I am in favor of strict enforcement of laws
no matter what." "It is never right to disobey the government."
"More than anything else, it is good hard work that makes life
worthwhile." On the Autonomy scale of the Omnibus Personality
Inventory (OPI), 58 percent of the new students, but only 15 percent of traditional college students, indicate that they respect the
authority of American institutions and that they agree with state-
ments that make virtues of hard work and determination.[2]

---

[1] See K. P. Cross, *Beyond the Open Door: New Students to Higher
Education* (San Francisco: Jossey-Bass, 1971).
[2] See K. P. Cross, "New Students of the '70s," *Research Reporter,*
1971, *6*(4), p. 3.

If we take them at their word, the new college students are willing to work hard, but they want an education that prepares them for the practical realities of life. Most of the students entering college through open-door admissions policies recognize the need for improving basic skills and study techniques. But they want more from their education than remediation of academic deficiencies. They want college to do for them what they observe that it has done for college graduates of the past—give them an entrée to higher occupational status. They are, for example, four times as likely to prefer a college described as strongly and specifically vocational as they are to endorse a college fitting the common stereotype of a good liberal-arts college with a high press for intellectual and cultural pursuits.[3] In a similar vein, we find that 72 percent of the freshman students attending open-door colleges across the country, compared with 44 percent of the students in private universities, think that the "chief benefit of college is monetary."[4] Quite simply, the point of a college education for first-generation college students is upward mobility, socially and economically. If college learning experiences can open new vistas and awaken new aspirations, so much the better. But experimentation and innovation are likely to be valued because they speak to needs—not because they represent progressive change for its own sake.

In light of the characteristics of these new students, it would appear that the colleges that open their doors to the egalitarian era must establish their own distinctive criteria for excellence, seeking not to shape new students in the image of traditional students but to grow out of the culture of rural and blue-collar America and to create the education that will meet these new students where they are and take them where they want to go. La Guardia and Alice Lloyd have tried to do just that.

La Guardia recognized that the work ethic plays a powerful role in the value system of the local community, and that further schooling would have to compete with the attraction of money in the pockets of potential students. What better solution than to

---

[3] Cross, "New Students of the '70s."

[4] American Council on Education, Office of Research, *The American Freshman: National Norms for Fall 1972* (Washington, D.C.: American Council on Education, 1972).

assure parents that their children were receiving a practical education that would equip them for the world of work while at the same time helping students earn some money?

Although cooperative education is not widespread in community colleges, it offers the following advantages: (1) Students from the lower socioeconomic classes usually have had more experience in the concrete learning offered by cooperative education than in the abstract symbolism used so extensively in academic learning. (2) Students who grow up in constricted cultural environments have little chance to observe a broad range of career opportunities. The experience of working in different types of jobs, of exploring and "trying on" new job options, helps to broaden perspectives and to build self-confidence in performing unfamiliar tasks. (3) The overwhelming motivation of lower socioeconomic youth in going to college is to gain upward mobility. The way to a better life than that of their parents is to get a better job. And the way to better jobs, in their eyes, is quite clearly a better education. Thus, these students are ready and motivated to learn about jobs. (4) A major barrier to college for students whose parents exist on the brink of poverty is, of course, financial. It is not only the cost of fees, books, and transportation that causes problems, but looming even larger is the forgone income that a seventeen year old could be earning. Earning while learning has an obvious appeal and serves a real need. (5) A college oriented around the concept of cooperative education is likely to keep its roots firmly grounded in the community. Its faculty will have to keep up with changing job requirements. Employers and workers in the community can take a personal interest in the education of their youth. The ivory tower has frequently denied talented lay teachers the opportunity to teach. Cooperative education, true to its name, requires the cooperation of many people. The involvement of the community aids in their understanding of and support for education. (6) Some of these students will find themselves, perhaps for the first time in their lives, performing well in school—on their cooperative job assignment. Such an experience undoubtedly will do more to establish self-confidence and self-esteem than many a counseling session.

For all these reasons, the innovation of cooperative education at La Guardia Community College must be regarded as a highly

significant experiment in educational reform. It is a beautiful
example of the design of an educational program geared to the
backgrounds and needs of students.

The educational program at Alice Lloyd College also grows
out of the needs of the local community. One of the major needs
of youth in rural Kentucky is greater exposure to the world beyond
the hollows and small towns. Thus, much attention is given to building the bridges between the familiar and the unfamiliar. A member of
the college choir may travel farther than anyone in the family has
ever gone to see and experience things unknown to the previous
generation. In addition, Alice Lloyd's plan to mix outsiders into
the relatively homogeneous student body will enrich the environment
through the gradual infusion of new attitudes and values into the
familiar framework of the mountain culture.

Effective bridges, however, must be firmly anchored at either
end. Many students newly making their way into colleges come from
rich and distinctive cultures. America's earlier melting-pot philosophy conveyed the impression that the sooner a different culture
could be made indistinguishable from the majority culture, the
better off we all would be. But more recently the goal of cultural
pluralism has been to eliminate the feelings of inferiority associated
with being different and to substitute feelings of pride in being able
to make a unique contribution. Black culture, Spanish-American
culture, and Indian culture have finally captured the public imagination, but the culture of white ethnics and of isolated white rural
America is still frequently regarded as best "melted" into an amor-
phous mass of so-called white culture. The oral history project of
Alice Lloyd College, in attempting to instill pride in a distinctive
culture, has much in common with well-conceived ethnic studies
courses.

As a strategy for learning, the oral history project serves a
number of purposes: (1) It creates an immediate interest and a
personal motivation for learning among young people who see no
particular merit in, for example, the more traditional and impersonal
English assignment of writing themes with an emphasis on sentence
structure and spelling. Learning the rudiments of written and spoken
communication becomes an intrinsic necessity rather than an
extrinsic requirement. History becomes a living subject when ap-

proached with vivid illustrations of personal relevance. (2) It enriches abstract classroom experiences with concrete action-oriented learning. A trip to the courthouse or an interview with an aging mountaineer integrates life and learning and illustrates that learning is a lifelong process taking place all around us. (3) It replaces feelings of shame and embarrassment about cultural differences with feelings of pride and understanding. The search for identity is a problem for all youth, but it may be especially traumatic for those who feel that they must renounce the past without any clear idea of the future. As field work integrates learning with life, so learning about one's heritage in the context of modern knowledge integrates the past and the future. (4) It involves the community in the work of the college. Like the cooperative education program of La Guardia, the oral history program provides linkages to parents and the broader community through students. Parents who have heard mountain stories all their lives are drawn into the educational experiences of their children. Mountaineers who are interviewed talk with others about the work of the college and are pleased to be involved in the education of their youth. (5) It builds self-confidence and self-esteem in young people who are typically shy and unsure of themselves. They must test their ability to gain the cooperation of others, to communicate their wishes, to attend carefully to the feelings and sensitivities of others, and to express themselves clearly.

Like La Guardia, Alice Lloyd College has designed educational experiences to speak directly to the needs of students. Innovation is defined in the dictionary simply as a "change in the way of doing things." But educational innovation requires much more than mere change. It requires a careful analysis of the needs and problems of learners and the implementation of creative solutions.

The educational solutions of La Guardia and Alice Lloyd are remarkably on target when one compares the learning experiences they have devised with the characteristics of first-generation college students as they are revealed through research.[5]

Both colleges have devised ways to make education more concrete and active. It is well established that the new learners want to learn how to *do* things. They have little experience and

[5] See Cross, *Beyond the Open Door.*

little patience with the joys of abstract learning for its own sake. They may discover that learning is fun and carries intrinsic satisfactions, but realistic demonstrations of applicaton are a necessary first step.

Both colleges have attempted to build self-confidence in students who have had great difficulty in thinking of themselves as people with important contributions to make. The colleges have each taken a value of great importance to the culture and have offered young people an opportunity to explore and understand themselves in relation to that value. La Guardia has provided an opportunity for students to test themselves in relation to the world of work. Alice Lloyd has helped students to find identity and self-esteem through a personal connection with their rich heritage while expanding their experiences with the world beyond the hollows.

Both colleges have built self-renewing links to the community. The strength of these innovative colleges lies in their rising out of the communities and cultures they serve. It is difficult to imagine a traditional college, with all the good will and counseling services that could be put at its command, serving these students as well as these grass-roots colleges. Like cultural pluralism, educational diversity is a difference to be cherished.

❧ 2 ❧

The New Adult
Learner

*T*he four anecdotal accounts of programs in this section have as their only common denominator a goal that is now centuries old: to develop new programs that will, in various ways, provide sound and defensible education on an egalitarian basis, denying nobody who can profit from the instruction but focusing attention upon those adult men and women in our society who have persistently resisted education or been crowded out from its benefits by other people more favored than themselves. This aim is sought in each case by the development of a new pattern of instruction, embodying principles or techniques not previously used for that purpose and often resulting in a highly creative approach. A thousand other examples could have been added, some of them very large, such as the Adult Basic Education program supported by the federal government, or the effort to help those who want to secure by examination the equivalent of a high school diploma. But these four accounts present interesting and unorthodox activities and, taken as a group, make clear the fact that both creativeness

26

and a desire for excellence are still being applied to that ancient ambition of mankind which demands that lifelong learning be provided for everyone.

♪ New York Institute of Technology ♪

Joseph Michalak

For fifty weeks a year Wally Nielson works as general manager of the thirty-five-employee Industrial Tools, Inc., in Ojai, California. Every night he spends two or three hours studying his books—on accounting, business, law, business statistics, and computer science. Occasionally he will listen to an audiotape of a regular classroom discussion or tape-recorded messages from his professor. Sometimes he will talk with the professor directly by telephone—during the professor's office hours.

Then he spends his two weeks of vacation on a campus 3000 miles away. His campus is the beautiful 800 acres that once comprised the Whitney, Phipps, and Guest family estates near the Atlantic in Old Westbury, Long Island, now converted to use by the New York Institute of Technology. He gets together with fifteen other students—from California, Pennsylvania, Ohio, and other points across the continent—in day-long seminars that are part of a program representing a distinctive collegiate approach to meeting the educational needs of adults.

Within the next two years of primarily independent study, Wally hopes to receive a Bachelor of Technology degree from the College for Craftsmen, a program carried on in cooperation with the National Tool, Die and Precision Machining Association. The program was the first manifestation of the New York Institute of Technology's corporate-college concept, which teams up the institution with what Stanley Moses and others have described as the "periphery" of education. It is the part of the educational structure that encompasses business, industry, correspondence schools, proprietary business and trade schools, military and other governmental sources, and various voluntary agencies, where more money is spent than in the regular educational system.

The New York Institute of Technology, in its less than two decades of existence, has been gaining increasing notice in the academic community for its career-oriented programs serving some five thousand students. John Valley, who gathered the basic list of the nation's external-degree colleges for the Educational Testing Service, says that NYIT is "the most far-out institution" he has seen "in the use of electronics in the delivery of education."

Grants of equipment and property by the Schure family led to the founding of NYIT in Brooklyn in 1955. Two years later it was chartered as a two-year college granting the Associate in Applied Science degree. The next year an eleven-story building was purchased on the West Side of Manhattan to accommodate fifteen hundred day students and five hundred evening students. The institute was chartered as a four-year institution in 1960, and three years later it began developing a suburban campus. In 1963 a large portion of the Cornelius V. Whitney estate was purchased to form the nucleus of the Old Westbury campus. Since then the Winston Guest property and four other estates have been added to the complex. During 1970 NYIT joined in a federation with Nova University, the small but prestigious graduate facility in Fort Lauderdale, Florida. And a year later it opened a campus in a new skyscraper building in midtown Manhattan.

But, like most institutions of higher education, NYIT has to struggle to make financial ends meet. Seeking out clients to keep its facilities going full strength, NYIT officials admit, has become an economic necessity and in part explains its venture into the corporate-college concept. "We seek to serve students of all ages not presently being serviced by institutions of advanced education," says William Smith, vice-president for continuing education; "and to the degree that we attract new students, we create an impact on our economic well-being. Ideas like the corporate-college concept can be the survival of some institutions—maybe even this one."

Within the last few years NYIT's Division of Continuing Education has worked out agreements with industry, professional associations, and a correspondence school to give credit for in-plant apprenticeship and home study. As in its more traditional daytime programs, the primary target population is one often neglected in American higher education: what Alexander Schure, NYIT president, describes as the "second- and third-quartile student who is interested in an occupation and is not going to make it to MIT."

After a year of meetings between the NYIT faculty steering committee and various training and personnel directors, management and labor education committees, the New York State Education Department, and the Educational Testing Service, the college has come up with the following programs:

In its College for Craftsmen students who complete the 6000-hour apprenticeship training program of the National Tool, Die and Precision Machining Association receive a full year of academic credit at NYIT.

Advance placement is given to employees who have successfully completed appropriate courses offered at the training facility of the Sperry-Rand Corporation in Lake Success, Long Island. Equivalent credit is given in courses accepted by NYIT. Where only a portion of the content in the Sperry courses matches the NYIT course, the additional material is taught either by the Sperry instructor, at the expense of the college, or by a college faculty member.

In conjunction with the Life Office Management Association, an international association of life insurance companies, NYIT accepts up to one year's academic credits for students who have successfully passed the association's examinations in the last twelve years. The credit goes toward a baccalaureate degree in business administration.

A modified weekend college has been created, in cooperation with the New York City chapter of the National Electrical Contractors Association, in which student-employees work four days a week and spend Wednesdays and Saturdays on the Manhattan campus. The employees are paid for a five-day week, and their educational costs are borne by their employers. Like the Tool and Die program, this program is designed to attract bright young men into a depressed industry for middle- and top-level management positions. On a trimester schedule the students can earn a Bachelor of Science degree in slightly more than five years.

Students who successfully complete the correspondence courses in electronics given by the Capital Radio Engineering Institute, a division of McGraw-Hill Book Company, can qualify for up to forty hours of advanced standing. CREI agreed to modify and expand its final examinations in line with NYIT wishes. Students can earn an Associate in Applied Science or a Bachelor of Technology degree through the same independent-study–intensive-seminar format of the College for Craftsmen.

In cooperation with the Airline Pilots Association, advanced NYIT standing is given for work completed in the industry's pilot training and education programs. The pilots must pass proficiency examinations. They can earn substantial credit toward a bachelor's degree in management.

At the Army Signal Center and School in Fort Monmouth, New Jersey, NYIT offers programs for servicemen aiming for an Associate in Applied Science degree; in cooperation with the American Telephone and Telegraph Company, NYIT also offers a Master of Business Administration program with a specialization in communications management. In the program for servicemen, enrollees can complete remaining credits for the degree in a variety of ways: through direct enrollment in independent study at NYIT; a combination of independent study and two-week on-campus seminars; or through direct service from NYIT instructors when and if a sufficient number of the enrollees are transferred to the same location. If nothing else is possible, transfer credit is accepted from other colleges and universities. These efforts are addressed to a common problem among servicemen, who, as they are shifted from base to base, accumulate credits at a variety of institutions without being able to earn, because of time shortage, a degree from any of them.

As might be expected, according to Dr. Smith, resistance to the corporate-college concept and its principles was met at several levels of the NYIT academic structure.

Many faculty members presented the customary arguments expressing fear about the academic respectability of these programs. Some decried the involvement of industrialists in curriculum planning, since many of the representatives from business and industry lacked the academic credentials of faculty members. The anticipated negative reaction of accrediting bodies was raised as a specter. Faculty members who postulate that a student can be truly educated only by attending classes had little sympathy with the innovative for-

*mats. Some of the faculty felt threatened by the imagined
prospect of their being required or coerced into changing
their instructional methods from the lecture-discussion orientation. Others became uneasy over job security. They felt
that the innovative approaches would increase the productivity of faculty members in working with increased numbers of students, thereby requiring fewer professors.*

A not uncommon summary of what often happens when change
is in the wind on campus.

Each of the corporate-college programs was presented to
departmental curriculum committees, then to the college-wide committee and the faculty senate. "These deliberative bodies," Dr.
Smith says, "often raised the same issues as those voiced by individual faculty members; occasionally new ones were generated. A
continuous process of leadership, persuasion, education, and per-
sistence ultimately led to the endorsement of these programs. Positive
modifications of the curriculum design grew out of some of the
deliberations."

The Tool and Die program has been the model for the programs that followed. It began in November 1970 at a three-week
seminar for students, who ranged in age from twenty-two to fifty-
three. While housed in nearby hotels—NYIT has no on-campus
housing—the group underwent tests, basic lectures, laboratory orientation, exposure to the metropolitan area's cultural and educational
highlights, visits to local tool and die plants, plus an introduction to
the textbooks, study guides, individually taped cassettes, and other
resources. During the year each of the students was in contact with
his professor usually once every two weeks, never less than once a
month. Each student had access to a tape recorder that he could use
to communicate with the professor when the questions involved
did not require rapid exchange. Otherwise, the communication was
by mail or during the professor's telephone office hours. Upon completion of study, usually for twenty-four academic credits, some of
the students took monitored final examinations in schools near
where they live and work. Others took their final examinations at
the second seminar, during which a second group of tool and die
enrollees was in attendance.

Wally Nielson, though generally pleased with the opportunity afforded by the program, has found other matters that he hopes can be improved before he becomes eligible for a degree. "'Ultimately the program will work better," he says. "But right now there isn't enough contact between the student and his professors. Some of them send mesages by tape recorder and cassettes, but others don't respond as rapidly as I would like. There should also be fuller elaboration of study guides with more personal guidance in their use. Even when tapes are being exchanged rapidly, the answer isn't there when I want it." Furthermore, according to Nielson, the system "aims you more toward getting a good grade rather than getting something out of a course. The lack of constant communication accentuates that problem."

However, Nielson says, the instruction is superior in certain areas, and "overall it has been an instructive program." He is grateful that he will have earned his degree within a four- to five-year period. "In my particular locale it would have taken twelve years of work at night classes for me to complete the program." He also likes the fact that he can work at his own pace, adapting his study to the demands of his work and his family. When he graduates, he would like to teach about small business in a junior college.

One of Nielson's classmates, Edward McCullough of Culver City, California, dropped out of the program after a year, but not because he was disappointed in it. "I had premonitions and doubts when I began," he says; "but they treat you like one of their regular full-time students. The program and the presentation of the material are fine, but it is hard to get down to the books after working a twelve-hour day, six days a week."

For Mike Manaloris of Mastic Beach, Long Island, the sledding has been much tougher. He did not finish any of the courses and did not attend the year-end seminar. "It is a very good course for someone who can buckle down and do it on his own," he says. "But I need someone to talk it over with to get a clearer picture of what is expected—especially in the liberal-arts courses."

In the future, Dr. Schure and Dr. Smith see a far larger involvement between NYIT and the corporate world. "We entered this area," Dr. Smith says, "because we saw student constituents that were not being served. We are providing legitimate educational opportunities for persons who cannot or will not take advantage of the customary program." Concerned with the economic survival of NYIT in a highly competitive publicly supported higher-education network, Dr. Smith foresees a vast expansion of the external-degree program—especially among the military. He says that programs are being worked out between the institute and the Department of Defense to set up learning centers on additional military bases.

Dr. Schure says that the military is one of the greatest sources of craftsmen and that the new institute programs will be an inducement for recruitment and advancement. He expects that the society will more and more be dealing with career clusters. "Our mission," he says, "is to train top-level support personnel." The corporate-college concept is one sound step in that direction.

Chicago TV College

Joseph Michalak

Television has become an important means of introducing postsecondary education into the lives of adults. It has been notably successful in opening access to the physically handicapped, aged persons unable to travel, housewives who cannot meet rigid campus schedules, prisoners, hospital patients, and those in geographically isolated areas. In addition, it provides many adults who are unsure of their educational potential with an opportunity to "try their scholarly wings" before being exposed to the usual classroom experience.

In recent years there has been a burgeoning interest in wide-scale television instruction. New York, Pennsylvania, and Maine are among a number of states that are moving into open-circuit television instruction on a statewide scale. The Maryland Center for Public Broadcasting, in cooperation with four two-year colleges, has created a Community College of the Air. The University of Nebraska has received a planning grant aimed at converting an existing nine-station educational television network into a regional State University of Nebraska (SUN), offering two years of under-graduate study. While these programs are in the planning and development stage, the most highly developed program continues to be one that has been in existence for almost two decades—TV College, a service of the City Colleges of Chicago, a municipal system of community colleges.

Since 1956, using two educational television channels with a seventy-five-mile range, the TV College has grown from 25,000 or 30,000 viewers for a thirty-program course to an "unseen audience" of as many as 300,000 persons for a course. About 90,000 persons have enrolled in courses for credit through any of the seven campuses in the system. Three of every four courses have been completed. An additional 80,000 persons have enrolled in TV College courses on a noncredit basis, paying one dollar for the study guides. By the 1970s TV College had attained a total credit enrollment equivalent to 800 full-time students. Three of every four enrollees are women viewers in the home, and the average age of all enrollees is twenty-nine.

TV College began, in part, with a $475,000 three-year grant from the Ford Foundation. When the experimental years were over and Ford funds had been expended, costs were assumed by the Chicago Board of Education. In 1966 TV College became part of Illinois Junior College District 508 in Cook County.

As is true of most activities that break from the traditional lecture method of instruction, teaching by television has not been greeted wholeheartedly by potential faculty members. As James Zigerell, the executive dean, explains, "One of the major problems faced by TV College has been getting faculty acceptance. There are teachers in my college who do not believe that any learning can take place if class enrollment goes beyond thirty. You can imagine how they feel about substituting an electronic image for their live presence. They have had to learn to adapt their instructional methods and materials to a strange and demanding medium. No longer can they hear the dutiful chuckles occasioned in the classroom by professional waggery or see the puzzled frowns of uncomprehending students in back rows."

Even though Dr. Zigerell is a strong advocate of TV instruction, he is also alert to its limitations. He states, "Only the zealots and hucksters, who harm the cause of instructional television, argue that TV instruction has all the dimensions of classroom presentation." But, he argues, there is clear-cut evidence that from the standpoint of results on examinations, "the excellent TV lecture, especially when enhanced by the visual potential of the medium, can be every bit as effective as the excellent lecture in the classroom." Studies show that the home viewer, older and better motivated, can consistently outperform students of college age taking the same courses in the conventional way. Comparison test scores also show that the home viewer does as well as, or better than, his on-campus equal in age. But Dr. Zigerell will claim no more than that the performance of TV students is not significantly different from that of on-campus students of comparable ability.

A TV College teacher is recruited for a year from regular City College faculties. The teacher's work usually begins in the summer. Besides preparing his lectures, one of his main tasks is the preparation of the study guide, which contains in its sixty to seventy pages a detailed outline of lessons, a list of required texts and readings, lists of projected assignments, and whatever study aids are deemed necessary. Then he does thirty programs, each lasting forty-five minutes, during a semester and is available for correspondence and telephone conversations, for assigning term papers, and for other instructional activities with students throughout the following semester, when the courses are aired. In heavily enrolled sections extra help is provided by other teachers.

When a course is repeated on videotape, a teacher is relieved of a portion of his normal teaching load to review, edit, and update the course. He is also given time to coordinate and supervise the activities of credit students during the repeat.

In addition to on-campus conferences, the college makes special arrangements for courses that are especially difficult to simulate exclusively with TV pictures. Language courses require that credit students attend seven 100-minute conversational periods, and science courses offer four-hour laboratory sessions on Saturdays.

Each home viewer has a bulletin that lists the dates and times of conferences and examinations. He selects the most convenient of four City Colleges of Chicago locations for his examinations. Conferences vary in number and may be either required or voluntary, according to the objectives of the course. In courses like English composition, which require frequent submission of written work, students participate by mailing themes to "section" teachers, who grade their work and return it. Section teachers, like all other teachers, are available for scheduled weekly telephone hours.

Residents of Chicago pay fees of $10 for eight semester hours and $20 for nine semester hours or more. Illinois residents outside of Chicago pay $55 per semester hour plus the service fee, while out-of-state students pay $50 per semester hour plus the service fee.

A TV College course costs about $48 per credit hour to produce, compared with $50 per credit hour to provide a similar course "in person." Costs are kept down, says Dr. Zigerell, because courses often can be replayed for a number of years. However, parts of every course are updated before each replay—particularly in the social sciences because of constant social, economic, and political changes. The introductory lectures of every course are revised each time a course is presented. If an instructor insists that more than 10 percent of his lessons need new material, the course is redone, with the same instructor or someone else.

Although TV College began with live lectures, over the years more and more of the courses were put on videotape. Now all of them are videotaped in color. "Videotape," says Dr. Zigerell, "makes for better lectures and programs. We have better quality control, and it takes the pressure off a teacher to know that any fluff he makes will not be etched on a television screen."

Dr. Zigerell believes that whatever or whoever is put on television should be something special. But he makes no claim that every television course meets professional and entertainment standards, and he takes sharp issue with those who demand this—especially in programs aimed at adults. "We should distinguish," he says in an article for *Educational Technology* magazine, "two kinds of audience for instructional TV": the open-circuit—or TV College—audience and the closed-circuit audience.

The [open-circuit audience] is highly motivated and eager to learn. Students comprising this audience appreciate the visually enhanced television lecture but are sometimes impatient with production ploys that do little to enhance the instruction, which for them is the purpose of the game. Many of these people like the classroom atmosphere. They are people who have been deprived of classroom experience during their lives.

The other audience—the closed-circuit audience [the slimmer, on-campus group at the Chicago System]— is another cup of tea. A televising of a mediocre talking classroom performance makes them feel they are second-class citizens, deprived of the in-the-flesh mediocrity of the conventional classrooms. . . . These collegians are simply part of the McLuhan generation that associates television with entertainment and slickness of production, aware that the medium has a rhetoric all its own. They do not willingly settle for an electronic simulation of ordinary instruction in place of ordinary classroom instruction. The conventional instruction does, at least, have an element of personal interaction, no matter how pedestrian it may be.[1]

"The pond for the standard credit course," says Dr. Zigerell, "is a small one that must be allowed to replenish itself whenever it is drained." To ensure a credit enrollment large enough to keep production costs reasonable, and to give home viewers enough options to fulfill degree requirements, TV College has learned that at least two terms must intervene before a course is repeated. Eight courses, replaced twice daily and representing twenty-six on-air hours weekly, are generally presented in the fall and spring semesters; three courses are presented during the summer. To date, the college has produced more than eighty different courses, for credit. Some of these are rented by other institutions—like the Maryland Center for Public Broadcasting, the Milwaukee Public Schools, and the College of San Mateo, whose president, Clifford Erickson, was the first dean of TV College. Some videotapes and supplementary written materials from TV College are also provided for an eight-week computer programming course designed to upgrade the skills of army or air force personnel stationed in Europe. More than 2500 servicemen have completed the course since it began in 1969.

Every year ten to fifteen TV College courses—including

[1] "Televised Instruction: Where Do We Go from Here?" *Educational Technology,* September 1969, pp. 72–76.

Shakespeare, College Algebra, Business Law, Child Psychology, and National Government—are available on a lease basis from the Great Plains National Instructional Television Library at the University of Nebraska. Attesting to the dominance of TV College in this field is the fact that in 1972 all but three of the courses at the college level available through the Great Plains Library were produced at TV College. Great Plains is now making programs of TV College courses available for rental or purchase in the new videocassette format.

Though many persons start with TV College, only about 350 persons—barely 20 percent—have received degrees exclusively through television instruction. About half of this total have been physically handicapped persons and inmates of state and federal penitentiaries. Aside from the fact that it takes a considerable number of years—often seven and eight—for a person to become a TV College graduate, Dr. Zigerell notes several other factors that help to explain the seemingly low number of TV-only graduates. The real nature of the TV College impact, he says, is to feed "external" students into the regular academic stream upon completion of the equivalent of a semester's work or so on television. To date, nearly 2500 graduates of the City Colleges of Chicago took an average of a semester's work through TV College. Some years, Dr. Zigerell says, the records of as many as 20 percent of the system's graduates show credit for courses taken on television. Dr. Zigerell's statistics indicate that 53 percent of the credit-earning students want to earn at least an associate degree.

On two occasions questionnaires have been sent to former TV College students who went on to four-year colleges. The completed questionnaires showed that the three hundred respondents had learned as much on television as they did in the classroom, and earned about the same grades. Almost all of them considered TV College courses better organized. Above all, they showed that, after starting in TV College, a number of Chicagoans have been able to go on to earn bachelor's and master's degrees and make careers for themselves in business and teaching. Students who took several courses were most enthusiastic—generally those who, like Madeline Moriarity, could not have taken college work otherwise. In the five years it took her to earn a degree, Mrs. Moriarity discovered that

TV College—rather than being a makeshift alternative to the lecture-in-a-classroom form of college education—was, in fact, the best choice for her. She had tried a couple of in-person classes in one of the regular city colleges, but they didn't work out. "I didn't like competing with a bunch of giggling freshmen talking among themselves. That was high school all over again. And there was just a lot of busy work, with little quizzes every day which the professors use to check up on you and treat you like little kids." Once she got used to the television schedules, on the other hand, "it was easy." She took advantage of the fact that each course is broadcast twice a day—once for day people and once for the night shift. "I used a little of each, depending on how the twins ate and slept and stayed healthy."

Mrs. Moriarity, who like 40 percent of the TV College enrollees wants eventually to receive a degree entitling her to teach, said that the clear course outlines provided by the college made it possible for her to complete twenty-three courses in four and a half years. TV College sends each student a full synopsis of each tele-course, outlining what material is to be covered on each segment, along with what reading is expected to follow the lecture. "There were no curve-ball quizzes to worry about," says Mrs. Moriarity. "I always knew that if I had done the reading for that week, I'd understand the lecture. In fact, the outline was so clear and true to the course that even when I missed a week's broadcast I'd be up to date if I just followed the reading. I didn't have the kind of pressure you would feel in a regular college. If the kids were sick a week or something else kept me from watching TV, I could read ahead and fit the given circumstances. It fit my life-style, instead of my having to alter my life-style to suit a professor."

Mrs. Moriarity went to the campus only to take her examinations at Southwest College (formerly Cogan College), where her records were maintained. She never attended the class conferences that are held periodically. But she felt that she had all the contact she needed. "If I had a question about anything in the lecture, I could get on the phone and talk to the professor. Every one of them keeps listed office hours, and every one of them was friendly and anxious to help."

Pauline Koop, a Chicago Northsider who previously had

taken evening extension courses at the University of Minnesota and the University of Wisconsin at Milwaukee, also found that she preferred the twenty-one television courses she took before her graduation. "The give and take that supposedly is so important in a classroom was usually discussion of stuff I had already grasped. Lots of it was a waste of time."

Jeanne Brachi, a sixty-six-year-old Chicagoan, took eight years to earn her degree after her second and last son had gone to college. She emphasized the time-saving quality of TV instruction: "So many times it is so difficult to leave your things at home and get on a bus to ride to class. Not only do you save time on transportation by staying in front of your TV, but you also save the necessity of changing clothes and the other preparations you have to make to get ready for class."

Recently the City Colleges of Chicago announced formation of a learning-resources laboratory, with TV College as its nucleus and Dr. Zigerell as coordinator. The laboratory also encompasses an overseas military off-duty instruction program, an advanced-placement program, and the credit-by-examination and independent-study programs.

In the future, Dr. Zigerell says, TV College will do more toward supplying special services for special kinds of audiences— especially an audience with more of a vocational and occupational interest. "By state requirements," he says, "a community college like ours should have at least 30 percent technical-vocational orientation. At present, all our regular courses have been aimed at the serious-minded viewers capable of conventional college at an acceptable and often high level."

In mid-1969 the college began producing a special noncredit series on vocational guidance and counseling through a grant from the state's Board of Vocational Education and Rehabilitation. The fifteen half-hour programs were aimed at an audience of high school dropouts who need prodding to enter a vocational program; prospective high school graduates with no interest in conventional college programs but unaware of technical-occupational programs in Illinois junior colleges; and viewers, young or old, in search of new or more satisfying jobs. Resource people from local business, industry, and state agencies appeared on the program. Wherever possible, the approach was semidocumentary, with on-location filming, simulated job and counseling interviews, and dramatizations. Videotapes of the series have ben distributed to high schools and rehabilitation institutions throughout Illinois. An open-line telephone service invited viewers to dial a number for information regarding job opportunities and training programs. In addition, funding is being sought for a series on adult basic literacy and so-called "coping" skills. Courses have been produced in child care, electronics, and law enforcement.

Given a new generation of students accepting television as part of the school, given a faculty that recognizes television as an instructional medium that is here to stay, given prudent direction and tempered enthusiasm in administrative circles, Dr. Zigerell believes that in the future TV College will serve more people in more ways.

Rural Family Development Project

Larry Van Dyne

The University of Wisconsin has made Madison a center of higher education with relatively few peers. During the 1960s the university awarded more than 30,000 degrees, nearly a quarter of them beyond the bachelor's. Yet just outside the Madison city limits in the farming country of southern Wisconsin, the huge, neat dairy barns and silos mask an ironic fact: fully half of the rural adults have never been beyond the eighth grade, a statistic that is fairly typical of rural areas across the country. For many of these Wisconsin adults, the higher-education system that Madison represents is about as personally useful as a pair of Broadway theater tickets.

Although the university pioneered agricultural outreach programs at the turn of the century through the "Wisconsin Idea," those efforts have not cut into the enormous problem of rural adult undereducation. Since 1969, however, through its Madison educational television station, WHA-TV Channel 21, the university has focused sharply on this clientele. In a federally funded pilot project called RFD (Rural Family Development), the university has mixed television, telephones, the mails, and home visitors into a promising educational delivery system for bringing literacy and new skills to its farm and small-town neighbors. The project has implications not only for other rural states that have similar unmet needs—and nearly all do—but also for the emerging efforts toward higher-level, accredited "open universities."

Specifically, RFD concentrated the full thrust of its multi-dimensioned program on a test sample of fifty people in a four-county area that includes Madison's home county, Dane, and three counties to the south and west, Lafayette, Green, and Iowa. Most of these participants were over twenty-five, lived on farms or in towns of less than five thousand, and had an eighth-grade education or less. They all were white—mostly of Swiss, Norwegian, and German descent—and most were politically conservative.

Although RFD's sample was small, it was drawn from a clientele that is vast by rural standards. According to the 1960 census (the latest figures available), 43 percent of the rural adults in Dane County, 44 percent in Lafayette and Iowa Counties, and 51 percent in Green County have never been to high school. Even though those percentages are high enough, they are somewhat lower than Wisconsin as a whole, where 53 percent of rural adults, or about 767,000 people, have not attended high school. Nationwide there may be about eight million rural adults with only an elementary school education, and in some states in the South and Appalachia the percentage of country folk in similar straits approaches or exceeds 60 percent.

As might be expected, lack of education and low income are closely linked in rural America. In RFD's four-county target area, about 30 percent of the families net less than $3000 a year, one of the accepted measures of poverty; and many of these families are among those with little formal schooling. "Low-income families around Madison are among the invisible poor," says a Wisconsin sociologist. "They are not concentrated in pockets of poverty like the poor in Appalachia and some other parts of the country. Dispersal reduces their salience, makes communication between them difficult, and creates problems for programs that attempt to involve them in community action to combat poverty. The problems of these low-income families are not solely financial. They experience a wide range of personal and family problems that are intensified by the stresses of accompanying low income. . . . The role a limited education plays in the perpetuation of poverty has been documented extensively." Often the undereducated end up in marginal jobs as farmhands or in small-town service jobs, or they struggle to make a go of a few acres of their own. Often they retreat into their own homes and never become involved in local activities; many times they are too proud to take advantage of existing social services, which they view as charity.

Early in RFD's planning, it developed a composite of its clientele, which it called the John Shaw family. The Shaws were intended to be used in a rural soap opera in the television segment of RFD, a plan that was later abandoned, but still they give a fair idea of the project's intended focus:

> *The setting is a small land-poor dairy farm located about twelve miles from Johnson's Corners, population eight hundred, and thirty-four miles from Danville, the county seat, with a poulation of 4287.*
>
> *The farm, which is somewhat run down, was inherited from grandfather Adam Shaw, now deceased. Mr. Shaw cultivates about 75 acres of his 95-acre farm. He grows corn and oats. About one third of his productive land is rotated with hay. John is cooperating in the soil bank and feed grain payment program. He keeps about three acres in the program at fifty dollars an acre.*
>
> *There are twenty milking cows, twenty-five pigs, a dog, and several cats on the farm. The cows average about 9000 pounds of milk each year. Mr. Shaw sells his milk at $4.50 per hundredweight.*
>
> *The farm is equipped with worn and outdated machinery, a 1957 pick-up truck, and a 1961 sedan car.*
>
> *The home furnishings are old and slip-covered. Washing is done on a wringer washer, and clothes are dried on the line. A new sewing machine and food freezer were bought on time payments.*
>
> *Mrs. Shaw tends a ¼-acre garden. The family's chief recreation is viewing their black-and-white television.*

*The Shaws gross about $12,000 a year and generally
net one third of this. John Shaw is in perpetual debt for
about $5000. He is a poor credit risk, having to pay about
18 percent interest on loans.*

Burt Krietlow, a Wisconsin adult education professor, laid
out some of these facts about rural poverty and undereducation
for Boris Frank, when Frank went to the professor's office in mid-
1967. Frank, who is now the RFD project director, was in charge of
WHA's "special projects" branch and had received an invitation to
submit a proposal to the Office of Education for some of the money
that would soon be available for adult basic education.

"I asked Krietlow specifically what areas were not being
served," Frank recalls, "and he felt that service to rural communities was weak because of a number of problems—transportation,
the adults' lack of time to get to small towns to classes, and the
pride of not wanting to expose themselves in their communities."
Taking Krietlow's advice, Frank worked for several weeks on a
proposal, which he finally submitted to the Office of Education in
December 1967. He asked for and eventually got funding for three
years under Title III of the 1966 Adult Education Act, a competitive grant section aimed at developing "national demonstration"
projects. The total package was to cost $740,000: $165,000 in the
first year, for planning; $375,000 the second year, for operations
including twenty weeks of the actual test; and $200,000 the third
year, for evaluation and dissemination.

Frank himself was a television man, having done everything
from setting up a station on a Carribbean island to working with
CBS in New York. To balance out his adminstrative team, he hired
two education specialists—Vincent Amana, an adult education
expert with wide experience in the field, and Steven Udvari, a
former Job Corps curriculum specialist—as associate directors.

As Krietlow suggested, RFD's target population presented
a peculiar set of obstacles to overcome. One of the toughest was the
fact that literacy education—learning to read and write—carries
with it considerable social stigma for people in their forties. "Just
to illustrate the problem," Amana says, "I remember a sign in front
of a high school building, a great big beautiful freshly painted sign

that said: 'Adult Basic Education Classes Meet Here Wednesday Night at 7:30.' Now if I can't read or write, that's the last damned place in the world I would show up, because I don't want anybody to know I can't read or write. I have spent my entire life keeping it a secret." In rural areas, where everyone is conscious of what his neighbors are doing and where pride makes many people avoid embarrassment at all costs, the pressures to stay away from literacy classes are even greater. "Besides," says Amana, "the adult illiterate is very fearful of that school building because it was in that institution that his troubles began." So fearful of exposure are some people, he says, that even identifying who needs literacy education is a major difficulty. Television, of course, is a perfect self-admission device. All a person has to do is turn on the set and he is admitted.

Another obstacle is motivation. "The functionally illiterate adult needs to learn to read and write," Amana says, "but the fact of the matter is he doesn't know that. He wants to learn how to do all sorts of practical things, how to buy insurance or repair his car. But his inclination is to say, 'Yes, I want to know all these things, but don't ask me to learn to read or write.' He has a list of priorities in which reading and writing are fairly low. He has come to believe in the society's prevalent notion that you can't teach an old dog new tricks."

Then, of course, there was the problem of accessibility. The rural population obviously was spread over a wide geographic area that was difficult to reach by the conventional method of setting up centralized classes and expecting people to get there. The driving distances in many cases were great and especially difficult to manage in the winter, when the temperatures in Wisconsin plunge often to under 20 below zero. Cars do not start easily, snow and ice make driving hazardous, and chores take a long time each night. In circumstances like these and for people with low motivation in the first place, adult education classes might easily founder on a low tank of gas.

In their trailer house behind the WHA studio in Madison, Frank and his associates grappled with these three main problems of their chosen clientele—their inaccessibility, their fear of exposing themselves to ridicule, and their lack of strong motivation. As they thought about curriculum content and delivery systems, they

settled on several principles: (1) The home—not the local public
school or some other community building—is the logical place for
adult literacy education. Homes can easily be reached by all sorts
of media, including the ones the project eventually used—television,
the mails, telephones, and home visitors. Home is a convenient
setting for the housewife with several children or for the father who
often wants to stay home after a long day at work topped off with
a round of burdensome chores. By remaining in his home the adult
also obviously can avoid parading his illiteracy down to those
Wednesday-night meetings at the high school. (2) The adult's lack
of motivation for reading and writing courses requires approaching
the subject through the back door, first giving him bits of information that will be useful in his work or around the house and farm—
his "top priorities," as RFD calls them—then coaxing him into
improving his reading and writing so that he can better deal with
those top priorities. To determine what these priorities are, RFD
conducted a survey of its potential clients, asking them to choose
from a list of 104 possibilities the things they most wanted to learn.
The items people selected most were these: living within my means,
what do I live on when I retire, smart food buying, looking for a
job, how can I become a better person, and understanding insurance. Nowhere in the top ten were such items as using better
English, increasing my vocabulary, writing good letters, spelling
better, improving my reading, or using math better. What rural
adults need most, RFD reasoned, is a curriculum of "living" or
"coping" skills. (3) Television—so well suited to reaching sparsely
populated areas and bring learning into the home—would be a
hopelessly boring device unless it went beyond the standard instructional formats. "Most people attempt to teach via television
exactly the way they teach in the classroom," Amana says. "Each
week for eight weeks I sat in an auditorium at a university in which
they showed a one-hour film of Linus Pauling standing in front of
a laboratory table in a lecture hall at Princeton University lecturing
on the nature of the chemical bond. It was the best sleep I had that
eight weeks." Similar use of television, RFD reasoned, would garner
perhaps the lowest ratings in the history of the medium. An RFD
poll discovered that folks around Madison were avid fans of the

nightly network news; Walter Cronkite was something of a folk hero. What RFD discovered in analyzing those shows, Frank says, was that they were paste-ups of short bits of information, a bit of film followed by a newscaster followed by another bit of film. There was usually something for everyone if he stayed tuned in. RFD decided to adopt a similar kind of newsmagazine format for its half-hour television show. (4) Television—while good as a motivating device—needs supplemental support if instruction is to meet the needs of individuals. Part of the individualization could be provided through home-study materials, which consisted mostly of short two- or three-page essays and picture demonstrations that were directly linked to the client population's top priorities. Because the materials were looseleaf, a television viewer could write RFD's Madison address and request any or all of scores of units that ranged from The Art of Listening to Home Sanitation. Because they were non-sequential, he did not have to worry about whether he was keeping up with the rest of the people in the program or even whether he covered the same material at all.

Still, the home-study materials and television could go only so far in helping adults with their very specific problems. They could, for instance, present a few pointers on "dealing with my marriage partner," but they were of little use to someone whose husband or wife was an alcoholic. These situations required more direct person-to-person counseling in the form of a once-a-week home visitor, who could reinforce the television, who could help with the alcoholism problem, and who could help people grasp the home-study materials.

To complete its system RFD decided to set up a feedback system that would at least partially overcome the fact that television is only a one-way medium. The project set up a toll-free telephone line to Madison, where viewers could call for advice or information on their personal problems and questions. This Action Line, comparable to that used by several daily newspapers, was staffed by volunteer churchwomen, who tried to get answers and phone back. Common questions were answered on the air.

It took more than a year to work out these concepts and then to produce the television show, write the home-study materials, and recruit a staff of eight home visitors, mostly women with a high school education who were drawn from the small towns and farms of the four-county area. Using booths at county fairs and commercial advertising spots alongside Lawrence Welk, *Green Acres,* and *The Andy Griffith Show,* RFD recruited a sizable following. Fifty people got the full thrust of the progam, including the home visits. But because the show appeared on an open airway and because anyone could write in for the free home-study bulletins, as many as two thousand people may have seen the show and received the materials. An estimated 25 percent of the four-county audience is believed to have seen the show at least once, an unusually high percentage for educational television.

A guitar player picks a slow, easygoing melody as the camera sweeps across a patch of Wisconsin's contoured cornfields, neat pastures, and trim farmsteads. "I suppose I'm pretty prejudiced," says a voice, "but isn't this an awfully nice place to call home? . . . I'm Jim Mader, that's the Mader farm out in Iowa County. We'll show you a little more of that in a few minutes and welcome to RFD." The RFD logo—a heavy outline of a farm mailbox with "RFD" printed just below it—comes on the screen, and an announcer tells what is coming up: "Today on RFD. Talk and song from the fabulous Johnny Cash. Tips for winter driving from *Good Housekeeping*'s Charlotte Montgomery. The secret of a meal in one dish from food expert Shirley Young. And a new way to get your questions and problems answered—Action Line. Now here's RFD Host Jim Mader."

A forty-one-year-old local radio and television broadcaster, Mader is something of a personality among farm folks in the Madison area, a kind of local Walter Cronkite. He has a friendly voice and speaks the language that rural Americans understand. He owns his own farm, and it was by design that RFD's first feature was on that farm, to make Mader even more trusted than he already was.

In his kitchen set Mader stands behind a counter and moves directly into the segment on Johnny Cash: "Johnny Cash is everywhere. You and I know him from dozens of hit records he's had since the late 1950s, from his television show that is currently so popular. He's one of the richest country boys around. But that's Johnny Cash the performer. I wonder if you've ever wondered about Johnny Cash the man, what he thinks, how he thinks. Well, at RFD we did, so we packed our cameras and went down to the Ohio State Fair in Columbus, Ohio, and between shows Johnny took the time to talk to RFD's Dave Prowitt." Cash then talks about his concern for ecology and says, in response to a question about what he would change about the country if he could, that he would help poor people more.

This is the opening of the first of twenty weekly shows (each repeated four times a week) that make up the television component of the project. In short segments—some that last only a few seconds and others that run three or four minutes—the television provides a blend of television personality interviews, household and farmyard hints, recipes, advice from experts on coping with government agencies, and trips to historical sites throughout the state. In the next twenty weeks, RFD viewers will hear interviews with Eddie Albert of *Green Acres,* Buddy Ebsen and Irene Ryan of *The Beverly Hillbillies,* Chet Huntley, Burl Ives, and Andy Griffith. They will get tips on how to save their fingers while driving a nail, how to use split garden hose as sled bumpers, and how to remove water marks from a table. They will get advice on legal aid, social security, health care, and septic tank regulations. Bonnie Prudden will show them a few exercises, and a travel expert will talk about inexpensive places to visit in Wisconsin. Near the end of most shows there will be a question and an answer from Action Line: how to keep apples from falling off trees, how to adopt a child, how to make biscuits rise. Also near the end of the show will be a plug for RFD's home bulletins, where viewers can learn more about such things as "smart food buying," "home first aid," and "family spending plans."

One of Mader's regular viewers and one of RFD's test group is Lois Johnson, who lives with her husband and seven of their ten children in a do-it-yourself, remodeled one-room schoolhouse forty miles south of Madison. Mrs. Johnson never made it beyond the eighth grade; neither did her husband, who supports the big family as best he can by cleaning and whitewashing barns. Mrs. Johnson's first encounter with RFD was at one of the project's booths at the

Green County fair. "I didn't know what I was getting into," she says, "but they said sign up anyway . . . so many are going to be picked for this deal. . . . They gave us a yardstick and some leaflets and I figured that was the end of it. We were remodeling and I figured we could use the yardstick for measuring windows. But then I gets a call that I had been picked."

During the next twenty weeks, Mrs. Johnson listened to Mader's show, she ordered and studied closely the home-study materials, and she talked every week with her home visitor. She especially liked the parts of the show and the home-study materials that provided her with household hints: "All your poisons was listed in there," she says. "It tells you not to mix certain poisons together, you know. There's a lot of people that don't know that when you put this here cleaner in a stool and then dump bleach in there you might just as well throw a bomb in there." She talked with the home visitor about the show and got help with the materials and advice about personal problems, things like the difficulties her children were having in school. Even now she keeps the home-study kits on her kitchen counter—next to the canning jars and geraniums. Was the project useful for her? "I think it helps people a lot that didn't get a chance to go on to high school. . . . Like one subject was on politics . . . and what I liked about it was that it all come easily explained. A fifth or sixth grader could take this and read it and he would figure out right from there without reading all those big civics books that we had when I was in school. Everything then was so complicated. You had a book about yea thick and you had to read it practically word for word or you didn't know what it was about. These come in little pamphlets and a lot of it in comic form, which was real simple and really enjoyable reading."

Obviously, one of the questions raised by Mrs. Johnson's experience and Project RFD in general is exactly where this sort of education fits into the American educational landscape. In content, of course, it is nowhere near what we have come to think of as the responsibility of "higher" education. On the other hand, if the higher-education system is, as some suggest, to take on the task of universal educational service to adults, it is clear that a large portion of the clientele has needs that are as elementary and practical as Mrs. Johnson's.

Advance Schools, Inc.

Joseph Michalak

About 5,200,000 Americans are going to school via the mailbox this year. More than 60,000 of them are enrolled in what one high official of the National Home Study Council calls "the most exciting school in the correspondence study field in the last twenty years." It is the Advance Schools, Inc., headquartered in Chicago but spread across 37 states with 125 district offices and almost 600 sales representatives.

The Advance Schools is a closely knit family. Sherman T. Christensen founded the schools in 1937 as a subsidiary of the Christy Supply Company. The vice-presidents are Sherman C. Christensen (administrative services), the eldest of three sons, a graduate in educational administration; Richard A. Christensen (marketing), a graduate electronics engineer; and George W. Christensen (education), a master's degree holder in electrical engineering. The president's wife is the majority stockholder.

Sherman T. Christensen started the company after he himself became somewhat disillusioned with the correspondence-study field. In the depths of the 1930s' Depression, he answered an advertisement for a course in sewing machine repair. The extent of the first lesson was to advise him to call on a customer and ask for the customer's instruction manual. Mr. Christensen thought that he could construct a more imaginative correspondence course than that. He began with a home-training program for the servicing of electrical equipment and appliances. This remained the nucleus of the school's educational program until 1960. In 1956 the company was renamed Advance Training Institute and two years later Advance Trades School.

In 1963 enrollment began in mobile engine service and vehicle maintenance, which was in development for two years.

Many of the students in these courses were not only able to operate part-time repair services but also went into full-time businesses for themselves. Aware that some students lacked the business training necessary to operate businesses efficiently, the school began programs in bookkeeping and elementary accounting and started the second division—the Advance School of Business. Advance Schools of Secretarial Sciences, Drafting and Design, and Electronics have since been added. In 1970 the schools were banded together as Advance Schools, Inc. Two years later the air conditioning and refrigeration section of the old electrical equipment course was split off into a separate course. As it became apparent that many students taking the electrical course did not require the complete training, portions were converted into short courses in small-appliance servicing, major appliances, motors, and electric wiring. This split-off also took place later with the mobile engine service course.

In the profit-making home-study field, pockmarked by fraud in the past, these vocationally oriented schools have demonstrated that they can meet the needs of their students and still turn a profit. Among the factors that make ASI distinctive in its field are the following: ASI introduced the full-salaried sales staff in the home-study field, to cut down on the possiblity of sales misrepresentation. It charges only for what study a student completes. For an operation of its size, it has achieved one of the highest completion-of-course rates in its field: about 70 percent of the enrollees. It maintains by far the highest rate of rejection of potential students: 15 to 20 percent, compared with a customary 1 or 2 percent rate in other proprietary schools. Yet its annual enrollment in 1972 was fifteen times greater than in 1969, when most of the administrative changes had begun to take effect.

According to the National Home Study Council, the largest purveyors of correspondence courses are the federal government and military organizations, totaling about 2,250,000 students a year. These are closely followed by the 2,150,000 in private correspondence schools. Colleges and universities account for about 325,000 students, religious organizations for slightly more, and business and industry for about 75,000.

These "poor man's schools" enroll students of all ages, occupations, and courses of study. But the students have one thing in common: a vocational purpose, learning to earn. Most of them hope to climb up the civilian or military job ladders, enter a new occupation, learn a new work skill, or update their training to keep pace with technological change. The 15,000 courses of study on the market cover everything from accounting to welding to auto body repair, from carpentry to professional writing, from plastering to traffic management. But in many cases the would-be accountants, carpenters, welders, and writers soon learn that one way or another they have been bilked and nothing else.

As a recent study entitled *Correspondence Instruction in the United States* (New York: McGraw-Hill, 1968), underwritten by the Carnegie Corporation of New York, emphasizes: "The correspondence instruction market is wide open to fraudulent operators. Anyone or any group can become a correspondence instruction supplier." The greatest danger is among the private home-study schools. "When profit is the main objective," the Carnegie Corporation report notes, "the risk of fraudulent operation is high." Among the frauds are "diploma mills," which award worthless certificates like Doctor of Philosophy degrees after courses lasting a few months. Some schools sell enrollments and offer no lessons at all. Some run Help Wanted advertisements as a come-on for prospective students. The Federal Trade Commission receives countless complaints from students misled by sales pitches and tricky contract provisions for cancellations and refunds of fees and tuition. The contracts are commonly sold to third parties, leaving students without legal defense when they want to drop the course or the school does not live up to its bargain.

During the latter half of the 1960s more than sixty individuals were convicted of using the mails to defraud students. An average of four million dollars was spent by students at schools that were convicted of fraud or that discontinued operations before possible conviction. Not so the Advance Schools. ASI is one of the most active schools in the National Home Study Council, a trade organization designed to build public trust and to promote sound standards and ethical standards among its members. "The biggest problem in the home-study field is credibility," says Sherman C. Christensen, ASI vice-president. "There are many good schools, but because of the schlock operations, there is a lot of distaste about the field in general." In fact, it was misrepresentation about some aspects of the Advance Schools by commission salesmen on its Pennsylvania staff that led Sherman T. Christensen, founder and president of the school, to decide in 1968 to employ a full-time salaried sales staff. "When you have an independent contractor who is interested in a fast commission, it's to hell with service and follow-up with a student," Sherman C. Christensen, his eldest son, says. "He might oversell what the program will do for a student in career choice and income, or misrepresent refund policies. We could end up with a disgusted student. Our new salaried full-time salesmen are corporate people, interested in the progress of the corporation. They are instructed, if one of our students gets behind in his work, to see what's wrong and get him whatever help he needs."

Once a student's application is submitted and tuition forwarded, a fifteen-day cooling-off period ensues, during which either the student or the school can cancel the agreement. On the basis of a test lesson and an examination during this period, the schools determine whether the student can handle the work. "We would like to accept every person that applies to us for training," the president of ASI says, "but we cannot conscientiously do so. Some courses require special backgrounds in mathematics and at least a high school education. Also, some people would not make good mechanics and it would be an injustice to accept an enrollment from a person in a program he could not handle."

Out of 62,000 applications processed during 1972, Advance Schools rejected 9000—almost 15 percent. In the previous two years the rejection rates were 24 percent in 1970 and 15 percent in 1971. "That is unheard of in the home-study field," says Henry Q. Wellman, administrative assistant for the National Home Study Council; 1 or 2 percent is a high rejection rate in this business." According to Sherman C. Christensen, "You could count on the fingers of one hand the number of home-study schools that have a strong rejection policy. Most of them reject merely on the basis that a student cannot pay for his course." Of those rejected by ASI, only 20 percent are rejected for inability to meet payments.

Going hand in hand with careful selection of students at ASI is a high percentage of completion of courses by the students. An outside study of students enrolled between July 1968 and

October 1969 showed that as of April 30, 1971, 45.4 percent of the students in the three major vocational courses had graduated, and 20 percent were still active in the course; 12.5 percent were still enrolled though not active, and 21 percent had dropped out. Wellman, who hopes that the trends being set by ASI will become commonplace in the home-study field, says that the customary range of completion of courses in the fields comparable to those offered at ASI is from 35 percent to 40 percent. One correspondence school, the American Medical Records Association, claims a higher completion record, but its course lasts only a few weeks and has a higher-level student than is characteristic of vocational courses.

Advance Schools courses are designed to take a maximum of two years. After that period the student can elect to stay in the course or drop out with a refund for work not completed. Most vocational students complete the courses in from fifteen to eighteen months. Under the new accreditation regulations of the Home Study Council, a school is entitled to get full tuition from anyone who drops out after completing more than half a course. But Advance collects only by the lesson, plus an initial $70 charge. "There are only a few other proprietary schools that operate this way," says Sherman C. Christensen.

A student does not graduate without effort. He can be dropped if he fails to complete a minimum of four lessons a month, without permission from his instructor, or if more than 15 percent of the lessons he takes are failed. "This doesn't happen too often" says Christensen. "We will tutor the student if we have to. If a student scores less than 70 percent on his lessons by the time the course ends, he has to be satisfied with a certificate of completion. ASI diplomas go only to those who maintain an average of 70 percent or higher."

In addition to a general catalog of its services, ASI sends each student who enrolls a booklet outlining course objectives, the lessons and schedules for return of tests, and a description of the kits included in the tuition. The objective of the course in electric service and appliance repair, for example, is to "enable the ASI student to develop into a specialty technician, a foreman, or a service manager. With sales ability he could advance to parts manager, salesman, or manage his own business in appliance repair, commercial and residential wiring, motor-generator repair and maintenance." The sixty lessons, with a study and laboratory equivalency for 810 hours, provide for fifteen kits, which include such materials as soldering equipment, toolbox, set of screwdrivers, vacuum gauge, components to build an ohmmeter, and a professional-service sign for outside mounting as part of developing a profitable electrical service and repair business. The course costs $990.

Based on feedback from students on inappropriate material, Advance Schools revises its courses where necessary every six to eight months.

Some of the kits that ASI sends also contain many audio-visual devices. These include recordings, in which instructors talk to the student about how to do a specific assignment, as well as filmstrips demonstrating difficult concepts and the use and repair of complex mechanisms.

Shipment of lessons is computerized. In the automotive course, for example, the ninth lesson in a shipment is a "trigger" lesson. If after the twelfth lesson the test that goes with the triggered lesson has not been returned by the student, the ASI field staff acts through letters, phone calls, and personal visits to prevent the student from dropping out. The grading of the tests is also computerized, so that 38,000 tests are graded and returned each week.

Sherman C. Christensen ascribes the "fantastic" expansion of ASI in recent years to "the greatly expanded and better-trained marketing force and the quality of the whole program—the courses, the services, the works." He declines to discuss the financial condition of ASI.

Who are the graduates of the Advance Schools? What do they think of the training they received? In 1971 Market Facts, a market-research firm in Chicago, was commissioned to find out. From a list of 600 graduates who had received the assistance of Advance Schools in obtaining bank loans to finance their education, 491 were contacted in telephone interviews. Five of every eight were between the ages of 26 and 35, two of every eight were between 36 and 45, and most of the remainder were 25 and under. Sixty-five percent of them were high school graduates, and 1 percent were college graduates; 7 percent had gone to college but did not graduate, and 22 percent had gone to high school but did not graduate; 5 percent had not gone beyond elementary school. Two thirds of the respondents had incomes below $10,000 (18 percent below $7500 and 48 percent between $7500 and $10,000). In the group earning more than $10,000, 27 percent totaled between $10,000 and $14,999. Four percent earned more than $15,000.

Why did they get into ASI programs? By far the largest number, 72 percent, reported that they had enrolled to learn a completely new skill. The remaining 28 percent indicated that they had had some training in the field they chose to study. Almost half of the respondents cited retirement-income supplement as a reason for enrolling, one third cited promotion advancement, and one sixth listed job security as a reason.

Of what value was the training? Although only 16 percent cited job security as a reason for starting in the program, 23 percent reported that their job security had increased very much and 36 percent said that it had increased somewhat. (It must be borne in mind that 72 percent were studying in new fields.)

Of the 230 persons who had received salary increases since their graduation from ASI, about half cited the skills learned during the course as part reason for the increase. Twelve percent felt that the increase was totally attributable to their school training; 20 percent, for one fourth of the increases in salary; 12 percent, for one half, and 5 percent, for three quarters. Since graduating, 2 percent had gone into business for themselves, and 1 percent said that this business was their only source of income. About one third of ASI graduates are using their training in their present jobs. Of these, 37.5 percent said that the training was very valuable, and 57 percent said that it was somewhat valuable. Asked whether they would recommend Advance Schools to friends, eight out of nine said that they would.

Talks with three of the graduates from Pennsylvania to whom I had been referred by ASI indicated that most of the claims seem borne out by the facts. The service does seem to be there. Each person had a negative thought or two about his experience, but the overall reaction was positive.

None of the students questioned had sought the training they received. Their first contact with ASI was through telephone calls from ASI sales representatives, who followed up with in-person elaborations on what the schools had to offer. Each potential student was an armed-services veteran entitled to G. I. Bill educational benefits. Each of them subsequently took the course in electric service and appliance repair. Richard Brown of Allentown said it in virtually the same words used by the others contacted: "I would never have taken the course if the Veterans Administration hadn't paid for it." Yet he, like the others, gained knowledge at no cost except time and effort.

ASI makes no secret about its enthusiasm for the G. I. Bill of 1966. One of its publications, summarizing the history of ASI, says that the bill "provided the school with a new source of students." Its three major trades courses and its bookkeeping course were all approved for tuition reimbursement for eligible veterans. So one should not be surprised that a profit-making organization actively pursues its advantages, especially if it provides value for its profits.

Brown, who was the most positive about the course, had had no background in electricity and had no particular goal in mind when he started. But he learned enough to rewire his entire house and to repair a refrigerator that went out of commission shortly after he had finished fifteen months on the course. When he fell about two months behind in his assignments, the district ASI representative called him "constantly to see whether I needed help." He was also called from the Chicago office. "They were all helpful," he said, "but not pushy." When he flunked the test on magnetism, the Chicago office sent him some explanations about the questions but did not provide the answers. "I still had to come up with the answers, but their guidance helped."

Like the others interviewed, he said that he had had no trouble with the shipment of supplies from Chicago. When he reported to Chicago that a small outlet in one of the kits was broken, he immediately received another one without charge.

Richard J. Hanna, an office worker from Bethlehem, Pennsylvania, was the most critical of the program offered. "For a correspondence course," he said, "it was OK," and the house-wiring section "was particularly interesting." But he expressed disappointment that the course did not lead to what he had hoped to get—a sound basis in electronics. "The gentleman who signed me up," he said, "told me that it would be good to get a basis in electricity first."

Hanna also said that there was "an awful lot of material in the course that he would never need." He also expressed displeasure about not having a teacher in front of him when he needed to ask questions. "It is hard to write to Chicago every time. So you say the heck with it, I'll let it go."

Andrew M. Resetar, an electrician for a general contractor from Bethlehem, made the same comment. "I'd rather have someone in front of me, showing me what was expected." But he praised the occasional recordings—about ten of them—in which instructors discussed difficult material: "It is hard to get interested in your work on a correspondence study when the kids are around the house. Having to listen to the records is informative, and helps take your mind off other things at the same time."

Resetar, who has had considerable experience with electrical materials, said that he had relearned some things he had forgotten since he had left the navy. He said that "some of the stuff was obsolete" but that about half of it was new to him. The section on house wiring was especially helpful, he said. He praised the service he received from Chicago. "They sent me tools when I asked for them. They were generally good to me."

Whether it's for love or money—or both—Advance Schools, Inc., seems to get its job done.

Commentary: The Motives of New Adult Learners

Cyril O. Houle

The first, and probably the most profound, conclusion of the reader of the four accounts just presented is that their success is based on the fact that adults of limited formal education will pursue learning programs only if fundamental needs are dealt with in a realistic way. The case is clearest with Advance Schools, Inc. (ASI), and the New York Institute of Technology (NYIT), where the vocational motive is paramount and the chief test of the program is an ability to earn a better living wage than before. Project

RFD is less strongly vocational; instead, the project was designed to enable semiliterate adults to have "the low-level skills they need to cope with the tribulations of everyday life." Among the four institutions the Chicago TV College has been least concerned perhaps with meeting primary needs, although its frontier efforts call for it to enlarge its teaching of elementary scholastic and "coping" skills.

It is in this effort to achieve fundamental needs in realistic ways that these four programs depart most significantly from the general belief of sociologists and educators that adult education is a middle-class activity, a belief that has long seemed to be borne out by both history and current practice. Matters were somewhat different before the beginning of the seventeenth century, when the only people sufficiently literate to learn usually belonged to the royalty, nobility, or the upper class, on one hand, or were cloistered priests, on the other. But during the sixteenth century, the spread of literacy caused both by the Reformation (which called for all men to seek salvation directly by reading the Bible) and by the proliferation of the printing press and its products gradually created a larger and larger group of people who had sufficiently mastered the capacity to read, write, and figure so that they could profit from the benefits of instruction. Despite the stern admonitions of such reformers as John Knox that every father, no matter what his estate in life, had the responsibility to educate his family, most of the new kinds of learners added to the old roster were members of the upper class and the newly emerging leaders of the upper middle class and their sons and daughters. The latter soon became the controlling group in adult educational institutions in terms of both their numbers and their dominant values.

But since reformers have existed in every age, the desire to carry adult education to the lower classes has been a constant theme in both history and fiction. In the long run, the record of success of such ventures has been poor. The evening schools which were first designed to give a basic education to those who missed it in youth have achieved their most spectacular successes in the middle-class suburbs. Patrons of the public library are far more characteristically middle-class than anyone wishes them to be, particularly the librarians in charge. The agricultural extension service (America's greatest adult educational success) was created to save the destitute homesteader from the consequences of pest and disease but before long was concentrating on the yeoman farmer, and now feels its strongest affinity with the well-established farm operator or manager, terms hard to define but connotating the possession of substantial capital and, as its members like to say, engaging not so much in agriculture as agribusiness. The number of examples could be extended both in this country and in any other advanced society. The same general account is repeated by novelists who have dealt with the theme, among whom Hardy and Tolstoy come readily to mind. Russian novels of the Czarist regime are filled with accounts of estate owners who tried to educate the peasants. Such episodes deal only with the visible part of the story. For every unsuccessful effort to reach the disadvantaged which history records, thousands of others have probably been forgotten.

For adult education seems always to have been one of those benefits of life which interlock with others in such a fashion that each reinforces the other. When an institution created specifically to educate the poor develops an exceptionally fine program, the members of the middle class first infiltrate it and then take it over as their own. The wealthy (both those who actually possess riches and those who have achieved a leisured ease by reducing their wants) continue to pursue the delights of learning by amassing libraries or using existing ones, belonging to study groups which are either elite or can be entered only after arduous preparation, going on study tours, and doing other kinds of learning, some of which is hidden away under obscure names designed to protect its exclusiveness. The great public and semipublic institutions and programs, meanwhile, are filled with the middle class, though occasionally a sharp-eyed observer will detect either a member of the upper strata of society or a determined blue-collar worker—or his wife—who refuses to be denied the values achieved in the great mass institutions of adult learning.

Even in the four new ventures described in this section, the motives of the students may not actually be as simple and direct as they at first appear.

Despite the clear supremacy of immediately practical desires in the designs of the programs, and their almost certain dominance if the desires of students were expressed, the informed observer also

may wish to speculate about other motives. Research in adult
education made clear long ago that the purposes of students cannot
be infallibly determined by the content of the courses they take. As
one study has shown, many people consider English a strongly vocational subject, 23 percent taking it to prepare for a new job and
45 percent to advance on a present job. In contrast, almost half
(42 percent) of those who study practical nursing are not seeking
an outside vocation but intend to use their acquired skills in their
homes. In virtually every subject, moveover, the desire to meet new
people is important; for example, it draws 21 percent of students
of salesmanship and 37 percent of students of foreign language.[1]
Furthermore, any one specific educational activity probably draws
adults with widely varying conceptions of education. The designer
of a program therefore would make a serious mistake by gearing a
program solely to one kind of student motive.

What are some of these motives? Of the many studies on
this point, the most fully developed is that of Paul Burgess.[2] Burgess
administered a skillfully developed instrument to more than one
thousand adult learners, asking them why they participated in
educational activities. The results were then factor-analyzed, and
seven clusters of motives were identified: the desire to know; the
desire to reach a personal goal; the desire to reach a social goal;
the desire to reach a religious goal; the desire to escape from some
activity or situation, including boredom or tedium; the desire to
take part in a social activity because the association with other
people is desired for its own sake; and the desire to comply with
formal requirements. Burgess had hypothesized the existence of two
other clusters of reasons—the desire to study alone and the desire
to comply with general social pressures. Although these two motives
did not emerge from his factor analysis, they might well appear
in other studies with other samples.

Let us apply Burgess's list of motives to the four colleges
discussed in this chapter. Although the desire to gain knowledge in
order to achieve a personal goal is almost certainly the dominant

---

[1] John W. C. Johnstone and Ramon J. Rivera, *Volunteers for Learning* (Chicago: Aldine, 1965), pp. 149–150.

[2] "Reasons for Adult Participation in Group Educational Activities,"
Adult Education, 1971, 22(1), 3–29.

motive in all four institutions (less so perhaps with the Chicago TV College than with the others), all of the other motives seem plausible as at least secondary reasons. This fact is true even with the use of individualized techniques, where the desire to take part in a social activity would not seem significant. For, as Allen M. Tough[3] has shown, wholly independent study is not widespread; people who apparently fall in this category actually seek a great deal of advice, support, and counsel from those around them. And one readily catches glimpses in the four accounts—taken as a whole —of the diverse motivations that guide these learners into activities, the one conspicuous exception (perhaps present but unreported) being the desire to reach a religious goal. These values are clearly secondary in most cases but may nonetheless be important.

The idea that participation in social action, including education, is based on a hierarchy of values, usually derived from the specific circumstances of life, is far from an unfamiliar one. Around this idea, in a now classic series of studies, Abraham Maslow and his followers have suggested a gradation of human needs, ranging from the most powerful and primary ones (such as hunger, thirst, sleep, sex, and activity) to the most elevated and lofty ones, such as self-actualization, a desire to know and understand, and a desire to enjoy aesthetic experience.[4] One cannot seek to satisfy the higher needs until the basic ones have been met. This idea is not new. John Adams, for instance, once commented: "I must study politics and war, that my sons may have liberty to study mathematics and philosophy, geography, natural history and naval architecture, navigation, commerce, and agriculture, in order to give their children a right to study painting, poetry, music, architecture, statuary, tapestry, and porcelain." Perhaps the current speeding up of social mobility, which widespread adult education has made possible, means that movement from one level to the next can come within a single lifetime and not require a progression of generations.

This process of educational advance may be facilitated by the use—by all four institutions, and others like them—of new

[3] "The Assistance Obtained by Adult Self-Teachers," *Adult Education*, 1966, *17*(1), 30–37.
[4] A. H. Maslow, *Motivation and Personality* (New York: Harper, 1954), pp. 80–106.

media of instruction and particularly by the vividness with which such media have been applied. The Chicago TV College has been at work for years offering sustained education centered on television instruction but also using especially designed campus instruction and personalized guidance. In Project RFD a multimedia program is carried to new heights—including a blend (not just an assemblage) of television, correspondence instruction, a telephone problem-solving service, and personalized visits by staff members to students—to reach a widely dispersed population of semiliterate adults whose only feasible center of learning is the home. ASI has been bold enough to break through some of the practices of correspondence education which have for so long given that field a mixed-to-poor reputation. It has also used the computer inventively to grade papers, to do much of the routine paperwork, and to signal counselors when personal attention to students' needs is required. Furthermore, it has constructed teaching materials which use a multimedia approach. NYIT has skillfully interwoven intensive theoretical study with apprenticeship, in-plant, and home-study instruction especially designed (as are its more traditional programs) for what the president calls the "second- and third-quartile student who is interested in an occupation and is not going to make it to MIT." In a sense, these schools are exemplars of some of the nontraditional forms of education which many national educational commissions are presently advocating.[5]

Such efforts to reach new learners have their limitations, and a close reading of the four accounts will find some points of sharp disagreement among the educators cited. It is clear as well that the new ventures may be but preludes or introductions, from which individuals will move to more conventional forms of learning, a purpose clearly in the minds of the operators of the Chicago TV College. Yet before many new adult learners are ready to enter the mainstream of adult education (as it is now carried on by such organizations as the university, the public school, the museum, or other institutions) and to seek the full range of learning objectives, they may need to be introduced to study by special efforts directly

[5] For the report most directly relevant to this issue, see Commission on Non-Traditional Study, *Diversity by Design* (San Francisco: Jossey-Bass, 1973).

designed to suit their needs and habits. It is equally true that the larger world of adult education may be greatly enriched by the introduction and testing of these new media and methods and by the perceptive judgments of those who use them.

In sum, then, it appears that in the effort to reach what John Adams would have considered a first generation of adult learners, two policies are important. First, the ends must be practical and the learning immediately rewarding, either vocationally or in other ways. Second, the means must take account of the actual life circumstances of the learners and go to them in their homes and their places of work; that is, a skillful, inventive, and persistently applied combination of new methods and techniques must be used to seize hold of the interests of the students desired and then to educate them by devising new approaches which take full account of their patterns of life.

♣ 3 ♣

Women

A single model for women's education would result in a grouping of disparate programs serving different clienteles under one umbrella labeled female, or its homogeneity would inevitably foreclose the development of a variety of educational techniques and purposes. The two programs discussed in this chapter, at the New School for Social Research and at Westbrook College, exemplify the trend toward a variety of diverse options for women. The New School is an unusual combination of institutionalized consciousness-raising in a businesslike context that emphasizes learning as a means to doing. Westbrook College is a traditional two-year private women's college with a unique delivery model for earning the B.A. grafted onto it. Both institutions are successfully responding to special categories of women with disparate educational needs. If and when women's educational needs are adequately provided for, these programs will be indistinguishable from those directed to adults or college-age students who for one reason or another drop out for awhile.

♣ Westbrook College ♣

Elisabeth Hansot

In July 1970 Westbrook Seminary and Junior College in Maine changed its name to Westbrook College. The new name

66

coincided with the arrival of a recently appointed president, James F. Dickinson, who launched a program to revitalize an old and very traditional community college. The new program is deceptively simple. For over a century Westbrook's charter has authorized the college to grant the bachelor's degree, and Westbrook proposes to do so—but without expanding its course offerings or its faculty beyond the present associate degree level. Under Westbrook's new program, called "Two Plus You," any of its women graduates with the associate degree will remain candidates for a bachelor's degree and can continue to study for that degree, at their own pace, at accredited four-year institutions. Dr. Dickinson explains: "Today's students have highly personalized educational goals, and too often they become frustrated with the built-in rigidity which accompanies a traditional four-year curriculum."

The program works as follows: In consultation with faculty advisors, a Westbrook student works out a plan of studies for the last two years of undergraduate work. She selects her own school and enrolls there as a special student; but Westbrook remains the mother institution, evaluating and controlling credits, granting degrees, and issuing transcripts. A student may wish to take her junior year at one institution and her senior year at another. Certain programs may involve residence study and work in foreign countries. Others may require internships, such as service in various offices of the local or national government or field service in urban and rural ghetto areas. These details will be worked out by the student and her faculty advisors. According to Dr. Dickinson, "We anticipate that most of the progams approved will involve successful completion of work by the student through enrollment in regular courses of other colleges and universities. Mere vocational experience without structured growth and learning potential will not be considered for credit."

According to Dr. Dickinson, the proposal won ready approval from the faculty and the trustees and, after some initial skepticism, was accepted by the New England Association of Schools and Colleges. "I've had less flak about it since the Carnegie Commission report appeared," said Dickinson, referring to *Less Time, More Options,* which recommended that educational institutions offer students a wider range of choices as to how and when they earn degrees. So far, the college has encountered difficulty in getting its new program accepted only in regard to teacher certification. Two graduates have been certified by the Maine State Department of Education; but, according to Westbrook's dean, "State departments prefer to award certification upon the basis of traditional programs of teacher preparation."

President Dickinson's view of women's higher-education needs would not be shared by many in the feminist movement. He points out that the new degree plan takes into account the fact that women have different life-styles than men. "Undergraduate programs designed specifically for women have never been given adequate attention in the American scheme of education. Women approach their post high school years in a manner completely different from their male counterparts. For one thing, some are under no particular pressure to earn a degree, and many times their education is interrupted by marriage. Traditional degree programs make no allowance for the woman who wants to begin attending classes again, perhaps after several years, probably at another institution."

What makes Westbrook's new bachelor's program worth studying is its potential for servicing the educational needs of a type of woman whose upbringing and style of life has a very traditional flavor. Westbrook students come from comfortable middle-class families, a large proportion of them Catholic. They are drawn almost entirely from the New England area, and almost half come from Maine. Parents, who are proud of having been able to give their children a sheltered, protective, and conventional upbringing, and who exercise considerable say over where their daughters will study, find Westbrook reassuring. The small campus of some fifteen scattered brick buildings is centered around a small, pleasantly shaded green in suburban Portland. The college's five hundred students are almost entirely white, and their education is expensive. (Westbrook, like many small independent colleges, has had to raise its tuition fees to meet rising costs). The basic costs are $3600 for a resident student, $2000 for a day student.

Westbrook styles itself a family-type college, and the atmosphere during orientation week bears out this claim. The faculty, many of whom have taught at Westbrook for a good part of their careers, greet returning students on a first-name basis and are prompt to extend the courtesy to new freshmen. The advice they tender the shy, often wide-eyed freshmen is sensible and reassuring. "Don't be too worried about not liking your new roommate; give her time, she may just be homesick." "No, perhaps blue jeans are a little informal for convocation, but a dress like you have on now is just fine and perfectly appropriate." The school has no drug problem, no racial tensions, no student riots. Few of the new freshmen, beanies firmly atop their manes of long hair, question the mild hazing that returning students subject them to. As one faculty member explains, "Westbrook works best for the girls who will blossom in an environment that is solicitous and noncompetitive. We give opportunities to women who would be submerged in a large coed institution." Two of the college's most important recent decisions depend on that rationale: the choice to remain an all-female college, where women will not be forced to compete with men, and the determination to have a bachelor's program available over any period of time for its "late bloomers."

Although Westbrook's unique open-ended charter was the germ of its bachelor's plan, other two-year colleges—after taking the additional step of applying for a revised charter—could copy Westbrook's program; and there are good reasons why they might consider doing so. For the Westbrook program permits easy access back to the university when the demands of home and child rearing have fallen off and the desire for further training—and a job— has become central. Furthermore, the program may be able to keep this alternative vivid and plausible for graduates through the traditional network of alumnae relationships and college reunions. There is a great deal to be said in favor of a format that allows returning students to plan a course of studies with faculty whom they know and who know them. The encouragement, the sense of not being yet another cipher, the help in developing an academically sensible sequence of studies, the advice about new courses or trends in their professional fields—all were mentioned by Westbrook alumnae as factors that made the new B.A. program attractive. By giving alumnae a base from which to operate, Westbrook's bachelor's program might be described as a university without walls but with a very strong floor.

As important as the sense of "home base" is the greater flexibility that such extramural bachelor's programs can provide for their graduates. The retailing or secretarial major may, five or even thirty-five years later, decide that she wants to go back to school in the liberal arts. Should she want a degree and the discipline that that course of studies imposes, she runs into real problems. At many colleges she is given minimal credit for her previous work. Frequently the polite disregard of her previous studies and the prospect of starting again from scratch are enough to discourage her from continuing at all. A Westbrook type of plan can accommodate and even encourage such a change of interests by treating the A.A. retailing degree as a minor and building the B.A. in history or in literature onto it.

The program also provides flexibility in the geographical sense. Kimberly Foote, enrolled as a major in elementary education, began her program at the University of Hawaii, where her serviceman husband was stationed. After a semester, her husband was transferred to Maine, and she was able to continue there at the state university. Another service wife accumulated credits at an extension branch of the University of Maryland in Iceland, and a third student enrolled for the equivalent of her senior year at the University of Massachusetts at Amherst, after completion of the junior-year requirements at Schiller College in Paris.

A different variation on the same theme occurs for the woman who intends to go on in her own field. Requirements vary so widely, both for courses within a field and for distribution requirements outside it, that she often finds herself planning the equivalent of five or six years' work to get a B.A., while hoping desperately that her family will not move to a new location, forcing her to begin the obstacle course all over again.

Finally, more educators are beginning to acknowledge that there is nothing sacred about the B.A. pattern of two years of general courses followed by specialization in a major. Why not the option to specialize first and leave the general courses until later? It can be a satisfying format for persons who want a particular expertise and the work experience that it can open up. And it is a particularly apt solution for women for whom a marketable skill is security for their family life, or for its possible breakup. Returning veterans have shown that liberal-arts courses work extremely well for those whose experience outside the classroom gives them a focus against which to test abstractions, and older women returning to college can be expected to have a similar grounding. While in theory any four-year college could start such a program, the control that subject-oriented departments exercise over degree requirements makes it more realistic to look to colleges without already established patterns and vested interests in four-year programs to provide this much-needed flexibility.

How would such an extended B.A. program work? Westbrook's returning alumnae offer several possible examples. Cynthia Walsh is a slender, stylishly dressed young woman who got her associate degree in applied science at Westbrook in 1968. After Westbrook, Cynthia enrolled in a one-year executive-training program at Jordan Marsh department store in Boston. Westbrook will give her course credit toward the bachelor's degree for that program. The following year she worked at Jordan Marsh in Portland, where her husband was finishing a B.S. in business administration at the University of Maine. That same year Cynthia taught a textile course at Westbrook as a substitute teacher and discovered that what she really wanted was to teach retailing. "A teacher needs practical experience, so that what she teaches hangs together. It makes a better class when I can give my own illustrations, and the students get more out of it also." The next year Cynthia worked full time as a department manager at Jordan Marsh, supervising from seven to fifty employees. With her Westbrook advisor she designed a program of studies in retailing which allowed her to earn her B.S. in retailing education after completing sixteen semester courses at the University of Maine at Portland, where she enrolled as a special student. Had she not already received six credits for her training program at Jordan Marsh, Cynthia's teaching experience at Westbrook would have been counted for credits toward the B.A.

Westbrook is cautious about giving too many credits for work experience; in theory a student can earn up to nine credits, but so far none have been granted more than six. "The program," according to Cynthia, "was a godsend. The University of Maine at Portland doesn't have a B.S. program in retailing, so I would have had to go into its business administration program and that would have meant losing about a year of credits for my retailing courses at Westbrook." As it is, Cynthia was forced to do some backtracking. She found that some of the courses she had planned to take at the university were not open to her. "My human performance course had psychology as a prerequisite. I had the equivalent of that course training at Jordan Marsh, but the instructor wouldn't accept it as equivalent. He could have checked with the store manager or even given me an exam, but I guess he didn't think that was as good as taking the course in his department."

Cynthia's experience points to some problems that the new B.A. program is facing. Because Westbrook students do not have to enroll as degree students at the institutions in which they study, they avoid major requirements and the need to get transfer credits for their previous work. But as the Westbrook literature states, "Implicit in the plan is the faith that other institutions of higher education will want to cooperate with Westbrook in this effort." Faith may move mountains more easily than departmental chairmen, and Westbrook may find itself involved in some tedious negotiations if the programs developed with its own alumnae are to be made to hold against the counterpressure of other institutions' requirements.

Another graduate of Westbrook, Mary Fortin, is an intense and serious young woman. Mary won Westbrook's Blue Stocking Award for Literary Excellence and graduated with highest honors. She was almost accepted as a special full-time student at Bowdoin, a men's college thirty miles north of Westbrook, which has just recently become coeducational. Mary is married and has a small child; when the Bowdoin faculty found that out, according to a member of the Westbrook adminstration, they reversed themselves on the grounds that she would not be able to be an active member of the community. Mary is philosophical about Bowdoin's change of mind. "It's a good college, but I can get the courses at Portland. And at Portland I can go part time and get a job to cover my expenses instead of having to take out a loan." Unlike Cynthia and more typical of the Westbrook undergraduate, Mary had only a hazy idea of what sort of education she wanted when she came to Westbrook. She took some secretarial and business courses, then left school to get married. When she returned, she decided to be an English major. Her secretarial and business courses count as credit for the Westbrook B.A. that she intends to get in music-literature. Like Cynthia Walsh, Mary plans eventually to teach.

The Westbrook program, attractive as it is, presents some problems. To begin with, it is quite expensive: $500 for two years, although no additional charge is made for students who expect to extend their study for the bachelor's degree over a period of years. The college does not expect any financial gain from the new program; the fee will be used to cover administrative expenses and added compensation for faculty involved in the new program (a needed form of institutional moonlighting—Westbrook's top salary for faculty who do not head a department is $9500). But $500 added to normal course fees incurred as a special student at other institutions could place the program out of the reach of students with limited funds who might otherwise be able to study full time.

Another problem facing the newly initiated program is its potential demand on faculty time, Westbrook sent circulars to about 2000 of its active alumnae—and received 160 requests for applications. Of the forty-eight students now in the program, almost half graduated before 1965, the oldest in 1936. The dean of the college estimates that eventually about half of the applicants will enroll. The counseling and administrative work required is considerable, for the college intends to follow its students carefully. Released faculty time or added staff is the obvious answer, if the costs can be absorbed without raising the adminstrative fee. Westbrook, with a tiny endowment and budget problems, cannot afford to subsidize the new program.

Although Westbrook at present limits the program to its own alumnae, it does not exclude the possibility of eventually extending the program to other qualified students, once its own pool of candidates levels off. But school officials are wary of becoming a "diploma mill" or of "getting into the business of selling a degree." "Students without a Westbrook degree," one faculty member suggests, "should be asked to take some courses, perhaps a year's worth, here. We want to know the students before we plan their program with them. If we let in anybody, how can we control for the quality of the degree?"

A skeptic might question whether the bachelor's plan is more than a gimmick permitting Westbrook to augment its status by becoming a four-year degree-granting institution without too severe inroads on faculty time or college funds. But the skeptic would be wrong to neglect the development pattern of Westbrook students, a pattern which can be generalized to include many young women who find women's liberation militancy unattractive. These women concur with the traditional view of the sexes: they expect to be married, want to have families, and are prepared to move when and where their husbands' jobs require it. Most of the young women at Westbrook give ready assent to the view that family and children should have the first claim on their time and that a woman should not work outside the home unless her husband agrees. Such views make no headlines, and their proponents do not show up for May Day demonstrations; they are not part of the greening of America. Their educational needs may seem undramatic and even a bit old-fashioned by the standards of the 1970s, but they are experienced with no less urgency for not being in style. Programs designed along Westbrook's lines are worthy attempts to meet the educational needs of a nonvocal and nonvisible constituency.

New School for Social Research

Elisabeth Hansot

A *New Yorker* cartoon shows an ample, middle-aged woman huddled in the corner of her living room sofa clutching a tear-stained handkerchief. Her balding husband, hands shoved deep into trouser pockets, stands to one side gazing at her with a baffled, weary expression and says: "A course at the New School—that's your answer to everything." The cartoon is prominently displayed in the crowded offices of the Human Relations Work-Study Center, an interdisciplinary department of the New School for Social Research.

The New School for Social Research, at the northern edge

of Greenwich Village in New York City, was founded in 1919 by a handful of dissident Columbia University professors to offer evening courses for adults who wanted to choose what they wanted to learn without having to take prescribed programs. It was characterized recently in the *New York Times* as an institution "that has spent its first fifty years trying to cope with the problem of what to do for an encore." The Human Relations Center is part of that encore. It prides itself on being the oldest (twenty years) continuing-education center for women in the country. Since its creation the center has changed its character dramatically, from a leisure and volunteer activity orientation to a no-nonsense commitment to devising ways for women to get back into the mainstream.

Ruth Van Doren, director of the center, has a clear sense of the need it fills. "The middle-class woman is suffering, just as the poverty woman is, for lack of productive work," she says. "And frequently she has been made to feel that the work incentive itself is shameful—that it reflects badly on her husband's earning capacity or on her own resourcefulness as a 'homemaker.' But this is changing. Women want an identity outside the family, and I hear an undertone in their voices that says, 'I will do *this* for *me, now.*'"

The Human Relations Center has about 1700 adults enrolled each semester and about 3500 each year; 95 percent of them are women. The typical student is a well-to-do urban or suburban woman (50 percent commute from the suburbs) anywhere from her early twenties through her late sixties. She is married, with 2.5 children, and motivated by the desire to get back into what she envisions as the mainstream of life. In good part because their needs are undramatic and not easily categorized, Ms. Van Doren describes these women as "forgotten Americans."

The professional woman knows how to get what she wants. But a lot of the women who come here need encouragement, support, and sensible advice. A woman may be in her thirties, recently separated, and trying to make it for the first time on her own. Or she may be in her late forties or fifties, with her children finally grown and with time to begin to think about her own future. She probably has had some college study and may have worked a bit on the side, but she hasn't really had important work experience. Her husband could be a salesman or run his own business; he earns a decent living and she doesn't have to work. Scholarships for this sort of woman are nonexistent, and there is little in the line of serious counseling. She needs trained help to focus herself, find out what she can realistically do as well as what she wants to do and, even more important, what is available to be done.

The center faculty, in the New School tradition, are almost all part-time teachers working in the professional areas in which they teach. They include among their number a senior vice-president of a public relations firm, who teaches a course on Women Moving Up; a former employment agency owner and personnel director, who teaches a vocational workshop where women are informed about career possibilities and shown how to prepare résumés and handle job interviews; a psychotherapist giving a course on human relations in the future; and a community medicine instructor from Mt. Sinai Hospital, who gives one of the series of intensive training programs in the community-services area. (Community-services courses enroll 300 of the center's 1700 students each semester.) The faculty, busy with their own careers, create in their classrooms a sense of urgency and involvement that maintains the center at a safe distance from the self-indulgent, desultory, "tea-time" atmosphere found in some women's programs.

That sense of urgency is reinforced by a work-study format that requires students to be active outside the classroom, breaking down the time-honored separation between learning and doing. The keys to this approach are the enrollment options and the course variety available to the student. A woman is allowed to audit courses before formally enrolling for credit. As her interests develop, she can go into the certificate program, then on to a B.A. The sequence is not rigid; a noncredit student can move into the B.A. program, and degree students can move into the certificate program.

A frequently traveled route for the returning housewife at the center is to enroll in the certificate program. Aimed specifically at the woman who has been out of school for some time, the certificate program allows her to explore new vocational interests or to prepare for advanced academic training. The program consists of ten semester courses, selected partly from the center's interdisciplinary courses and partly from courses offered by the New School, and an action project undertaken in the last year of study. The program allows a woman to tailor her studies to her special interests and pursue them at her own pace. Theoretically, a highly motivated woman could achieve this result on her own; but, in fact, many who have been away from school for a long period require the discipline of a set of related and sequential courses to test their ability to achieve the goals they have set for themselves.

Central to the certificate program is the project seminar, undertaken in the final year. Its objective is to capitalize on the student's ability to design and complete an independent action project and present a critical evaluation of the work. Projects vary widely in nature and scope. One woman initiated a craft program in a new Montessori school. Another helped Mexican artists present a series of exhibitions of their batik and silk-screening process. A seventy-year-old woman organized art classes for the Widows Consultation Service in New York; another set up a replica of the Human Relations Center on Long Island. Summing up the program, Ms. Van Doren says: "Think of learning as a process, a process on which you eventually have to act. What we want to measure is the growth of the student's capacity to act, and that is also a measure of her productivity."

The certificate program sets no time limit for its completion, although the center recommends that at least one course a term be taken. While most women who enter the course have a high school degree, some are admitted on condition that they acquire the degree while studying at the center. The dropout rate is 60 to 70 percent, a source of considerable satisfaction to the director. "When they drop out of this progam, they drop into a job or into a B.A. program; that's what we're looking for," remarks Ms. Van Doren. "The center is here for women to use as a tool for a more satisfying engagement with life, not for degrees or certificates."

Just recently, the center has persuaded the New School to accept the certificate for thirty points of credit toward a B.A. degree. Ms. Van Doren is ambivalent about this achievement. The pressure for credit comes from students who want the status of a degree and the mobility it permits from one job to another. Moreover, many certificate graduates work in health or social welfare or in the schools, where state and civil service requirements frequently make credentials a necessity to avoid dead-end jobs. "Before we asked for credit," says Ms. Van Doren, "we used the certificate to try to break down the credentials habit. The certificate stands for a special training course which is competence-oriented, and we still think that recent evidence of learning in a mature student is the best evidence for hiring." Or as one of her associates bluntly adds: "We don't believe in all this labeling, credentialism, and degrees, but if you can't lick them you join them—to a degree." The price that the center may have to pay for accreditation could be a loss of autonomy to experiment. Credit for some types of experience, such as volunteer work or part-time jobs, makes sense to the staff, and the certificate program would be the most likely vehicle for such experimentation. But if the certificate program is tied to the New School B.A., the program risks coming under the jurisdiction of more conservative departments.

The New School is not taking the initiative in pioneering credit for work experience; the center, reflecting the interests of its clientele, is very much more interested in the idea of giving credit for life experience. Ms. Van Doren thinks the issue will be raised piecemeal by each student's making a special case to the dean. "That's the way change occurs in the academic world—slowly," she says.

The center is expensive; an average course costs $80; however, courses taken for credit cost $85 a credit. Ms. Van Doren is worried about the women who cannot afford the tuition and is looking for ways to reduce the cost. One way she suggests is through the College Board's College-Level Examination Program (CLEP). Many colleges give credit to students who make suitable scores on the tests offered by this national program. Ms. Van Doren has asked the New School faculty to point out courses for which students may earn credit through CLEP tests. She is thinking of listing these courses with the corresponding CLEP tests in the next catalog. She would, however, encourage women studying for the CLEP tests to take one or two courses outside their homes to satisfy the need to "get out"; she suggests, as one mode of getting out, small "listening groups" composed of women viewing academic courses on television.

Ms. Van Doren is concerned with widening the center's constituency. "What can you do for the bright secretary who needs more education but can't get released time from her employer to improve her skills? We need scholarships as well as better counseling and vocational placement help. Without scholarship funds we shut the lower-income women out of the center—and that will be our loss." The list of projects that Ms. Van Doren wants the center to undertake is long: "We should be opening up other training areas in the communications media, in the environmental field, and in the paralegal and community-action fields. Why not women lobbyists or housing inspectors?"

The insistent note of "me, me, me" that Ruth Van Doren hears from her students signals a change of attitude to be reckoned with. To this observer it seemed as important as any of the overt activity occurring in the center's classrooms. An unappealing refrain? Perhaps by traditional norms, but not when voiced by two gray-haired women who were taking a course in self-awareness and the awareness of others. "I'm a widow and am more interested in the lives of my family than in my own. I want to get out of myself and out of my family." Three chairs away from her the same theme was echoed: "I come from a large family. My life has consisted of doing—doing for my family, then doing for my husband and doing for my children. Now I want to do for me."

Commentary: Women and Postsecondary Education

Elisabeth Hansot

Despite the rapid growth of the feminist movement in this country over the last five years, there has been surprisingly little discussion of women's educational needs. There are at least two explanations for this lack of attention. First, the content of education has not been a primary focus of the movement, which has concentrated its energies on publicizing discrimination in hiring practices. As a result of their efforts, organizations such as Women's Equity Action League (WEAL) and the National Organization of Women (NOW) are becoming vocal and effective lobbyists in the field of sex discrimination. And second, when educational content has been discussed, a strong reaction against the notion that women have special natures or needs, particular capacities or talents, has prevented the development of programs designed specifically for women. When many of the women's colleges were founded, their mission of providing first-rate education for women was grounded on the assumption that this education would service the different social roles and life-styles appropriate to the two sexes. To continue to identify special needs of women in a society in which what is "female" is judged inferior or inconsequential, many feminists argue, is to give aid and comfort to outmoded assumptions and self-serving beliefs.

Despite its focus on access to education rather than its substance, the feminist movement has made a signal contribution to women's education in developing courses and study programs on women. The courses originate in various ways: student pressure for formal recognition of the insights contained in women's liberation material, faculty willingness to experiment with interdisciplinary course offerings, and administrators' support or acquiescence. The content of such courses range from the scholarly (The Women in American History, Northeastern Illinois State College) to the provocative (The War of the Sexes—or the Literary Mistreatment of Women, Dartmouth). There is little information on the number of women's courses available, but all accounts indicate that such courses are rapidly increasing.[1]

Whatever the format, their advocates claim that courses on women are multipurpose. They educate both sexes about the achievements of women, they elucidate historical and contemporary attitudes toward women, and through such knowledge they provide

[1] The most comprehensive listing of women's courses is to be found in *Female Studies I* (September 1970) by Sheila Tobias; *Female Studies II* (December 1971) by Florence Howe and Carol Ahlum; *Female Studies IV* (December 1971) by Elaine Showalter and Carol Ohmann; and *Female Studies V* (July 1972) by Rae Lee Siporin.

a basis for changing behavior. Action-oriented members of the movement have charged that those who bank too heavily on the effect of such courses in bringing about change are victims of the "liberal-arts fallacy," the assumption that understanding will change behavior. Supporters of such courses retort that their function is mainly to provide a forum for women to explore their attitudes toward themselves and their feelings (often negative) about what it is to be a woman.

Like the many informal consciousness-raising sessions that have issued from the women's movement, the more structured academic version aims to have women recognize the extent to which they have assimilated "male attitudes" toward themselves. When used as a bridge between personal experience and academic material, consciousness-raising sessions are a good educational technique, enabling students to sort out personal problems from those that are social in origin and to think about ways of coping with the latter. But when consciousness-raising is used as the sole focus or motive for group discussion, those discussions frequently founder in undercurrents of futility and self-indulgence. Florence Howe at Old Westbury argues that a learning environment which incorporates consciousness-raising, open-ended discussion, and a nondirective teaching technique require students to take and keep the initiative. The ability to take the initiative, to be constructively aggressive, is a special educational need for women.

The debate over whether women should be educated separately from men depends on whether and to what extent their needs are thought to be distinctive. Those colleges that have decided to remain female usually cite a better learning environment among their reasons. "Until women are really equal, there will be a need for a separate education experience."[2] And perhaps not surprisingly, the militant Chicago Women's Liberation Union, which offers courses ranging from auto mechanics to the female in literature, gives much the same explanation for the rigorous exclusion of males from its program.

Another aspect of the debate over whether women have

[2] Edward D. Eddy, president of Sarah Lawrence, as quoted in the *Washington Post*, May 15, 1971.

distinctive educational needs is whether piecemeal educational change will be sufficient to accommodate women's needs. At a Cornell symposium on Education and Equality for Women, Esther Raushenbush, then president of Sarah Lawrence College, was roundly attacked for her claim that piecemeal change, such as later reentry into the educational system, would eventually produce institutions adequate to women's educational needs.[3] Betty Friedan, president of NOW, remarked that such accommodating attitudes are part of the women's problem and lend themselves to merely tinkering with the system. She claimed that there has been a failure to face up to the need for basic structural change, but offered no examples of what such structural change might look like.

Consciousness-raising apart, women's programs outside university settings do not appear particularly innovative. Quite a few organizations, such as Catalyst in New York City and the Washington Organization for Women in the District of Columbia, are involved in career and educational guidance programs similar to those found in university extension courses. The Martin Luther King Center in the Bronx gives an eight-week core training program for community health workers in an open-classroom format; the students, drawn entirely from the community, are mothers with fourth- to fifth-grade reading skills. New York City Local 1199 of the Drug and Hospital Union runs a more formal program with similar objectives for its members out of four city centers. Local units of the National Welfare Rights Organization (NWRO) give courses in family assistance planning, welfare law, and how to organize politically. At the other end of the spectrum, the American Association of University Women distributes to its members simulation exercises (games that require role playing) on the uses of power in the community.

The independent programs are similar to the university-affiliated ones in employing a variety of workshop and counseling techniques to inform women about manpower needs or to educate them in skills in which they are insufficiently prepared. If the independent progams have any advantage over the institution-

[3] Sheila Tobias, Ella Kusnetz, and Deborah Spitz (Eds.), *The Cornell Conference on Women* (Pittsburgh, Pa.: KNOW, Inc., 1969), pp. 1–15.

affiliated ones, it may be in not having to deal so directly with two problems: graduate schools and credits. Almost none of the new programs being developed for women originate from or, for that matter, appear to have much impact on the graduate schools. The most frequently offered explanation is that graduate departments are dominated by research faculty who are oriented to their professional disciplines and derive their norms from professional associations or from members of their professional community. Graduate department faculty, who conceive of teaching as conveying to their students a body of knowledge and the techniques to work within it, are skeptical of student requests for independent study or credit for work experience. This skepticism translates into extreme caution when these faculty are asked to grant credit for courses in new areas or involving new learning methods. And many of the women's programs, were they able to get their courses recognized for credit by the appropriate university department, might in the process lose a good deal of the autonomy that allows them to admit noncredentialed students or to experiment with new learning techniques. It requires a delicate balancing act to get credit for unorthodox educational ventures without relinquishing flexibility and risk-taking ability in the process. Many women educators are not convinced that their eventual impact on the "credentialing institutions" would be sufficient to warrant taking the risk.

Many women's programs need funds to experiment with and expand their offerings, but few if any are attempting to focus and combine these often disparate educational features into coherent programs especially designed for women. Many of the women's programs have developed as part of larger continuing-education programs for adults or as part of extension progams which because of their lesser prestige tend, even when university budgets are expanding, to be treated as the unwanted stepchild of the university. But even if more funds were available for experimentation, it is unlikely that there will be any one excellent model that answers women's educational needs. The present trend (as shown in the two colleges discussed in this chapter) is to provide a large variety of different options in many different locations. This trend is an accurate reflection of a heterogeneous clientele whose needs and ambitions are as diverse as the population at large.

🦢 Commentary: Higher Education, 🦢 A Chilly Climate for Women

Margaret C. Dunkle

"Women's liberation is the best thing that ever happened to higher education." Reaction to these words, by Patricia Roberts Harris at the 1972 annual meeting of the American Council on Education, was mixed: enthusiastic applause, uncomfortable laughter, stony silence. The same mixed reaction greets the position of women in academe today. Many applaud the long-overdue changes that are beginning to offer women a fair chance in the world of higher education; others laugh in bewilderment at what they perceive as the folly of some "crazy libbies." Still others—both male and female alike—remain silent and aloof, refusing to believe that the current move for equality is of relevance to them. But, however uncomfortable the issue makes some adminstrators, faculty, and students, the "woman question" is on campus to stay.

Increasingly, institutions of higher education are being called upon both morally and legally to be a model for a society free from discrimination. Because educational institutions at all levels play a critical role in forming attitudes of women and men and molding their career aspirations, sex discrimination in the classroom is especially damaging. Apart from its wider influence on society, education has a direct bearing on a woman's presence in the work force: the more education a woman has, the more likely she is to be employed. Many argue that higher education has the potential—and even the responsibility—to exert leadership in developing the all-too-often neglected potential of women both as students and employees.

We cannot separate the education of women from the *climate* of that education—the treatment of female employees by the educational institution, the respect that women receive from their professors and peers, women's access to facilities and resources. In a broader context, Snyder calls this the "hidden curriculum"—the covert determinants of the learning process which "are rooted in the professors' assumptions and values, the students' expectations, and the social context in which both teacher and taught find themselves."[1]

Much of the social context of an educational institution is determined by and reflected in the composition of its work force. Girls will not aspire to become professors or doctors or lawyers or business executives if they do not see women successfully performing these jobs. A recent study by M. Elizabeth Tidball[2] confirms on a statistical basis the importance to women of female "role models." She found that the number of "career successful women" (defined as those listed in *Who's Who of American Women*) was directly proportional to the number of women faculty present in the achievers' undergraduate institutions at the time they were students. In fact, the correlation was a practically perfect +0.953. Clearly, the visibility of women successfully performing highly professional jobs positively influences the career aspirations of female students.

Although many people still assume that women will be wives and mothers first, and students and employees second (if at all), this is no longer the case. Now the average woman can expect to spend at least twenty-five years in the paid labor market. Over half of the women between sixteen and sixty-five are in the paid labor force, and the number is growing. More women are becoming students, just as more women are joining the paid labor force. Federal legislation now prohibits discrimination against these women. A brief summary of the provisions of these laws, with emphasis on the legislation prohibiting discrimination against students, provides the basis for understanding the specific issues which together form the educational climate for women.

A number of federal laws now mandate equal opportunity for women on campus. Executive Order 11246 (as amended by Executive Order 11375) and Title VII of the Civil Rights Act of 1964 mandate equal employment opportunity regardless of sex (or race, color, religion, or national origin). The Equal Pay Act of 1963

[1] Benson R. Snyder, *The Hidden Curriculum* (New York: Knopf, 1971), p. 4.
[2] "Perspective on Women and Affirmative Action," *Educational Record*, 1973, 54(2), in press.

requires that women and men receive equal pay for equal work for all jobs from maids and janitors to professors and administrators. Title IX of the Education Amendments Act of 1972 requires that educational institutions treat female and male students, as well as employees, equally. And the 1971 amendments to Titles VII and VIII of the Public Health Service Act prohibit institutions from discriminating in admissions to training programs for health personnel (for instance, in medical schools, dental schools, and nursing schools).

This formidable legal prodding is forcing institutions to review their treatment of women for discrimination. For many institutions the law provides the how-to-do-it manual for changes they have wanted to effect for years. Others comply only grudgingly with the government guidelines and regulations; for them, compliance with the law is an end in itself, and the issues behind the laws are lost in the shuffle. For example, according to the college paper of a large and prestigious midwestern university, the university's affirmative-action officer "indicated that the university has not had time to really give thought to the reasons behind the anti-discrimination regulations, but has complied simply because of the government threats." Similarly, Martha Peterson (president of Barnard College) has chided her colleagues for their inaction and insensitivity to women's rights and affirmative action: "Do you recall our distress the past two years over the lack of guidelines for affirmative action? In retrospect we sounded a bit like the student who says, 'Show me the rule that tells me I can't do what I have just done!' The intent of 'affirmative action' was clear enough. We could have written our own set of policies and procedures for attaining its goals."[3]

Most people have at least some familiarity with the employment issues that are of concern to women—such issues as equal pay for equal work, equal access to jobs, equal chance at promotions, elimination of antinepotism policies and practices, treating pregnancy and childbirth like any other temporary disability. Many of the student issues are less familiar and less obvious. It is these issues,

[3] *Women in Higher Education,* keynote address given at the 55th annual meeting of the American Council on Education, October 5, 1973.

however, that illustrate and determine the educational climate for women at an institution.

Until the passage of Title IX of the Education Amendments Act in July of 1972, there was no federal legislation prohibiting discriminatory treatment of students on the basis of sex. (Although the amendments to Titles VII and VIII of the Public Health Service Act, which became law in November of 1971, prohibit sex discrimination in *admission* to programs training people for the health professions, they do not prohibit sex discrimination against students once they are in the program.) The key section of Title IX reads: "No person in the United States shall, on the basis of sex, be excluded from participation in, be denied the benefits of, or be subjected to discrimination under any educational program or activity receiving federal financial assistance."

There are three exemptions to these provisions: (1) Religious institutions are exempt if the application of the antidiscrimination provisions is not consistent with the religious tenets of the organization. Discrimination on the basis of sex for reasons of custom, convenience, or administrative rule is clearly prohibited. For example, an institution run by a religious order could *not* limit admission to graduate school to members of one sex because of tradition. It could, however, limit faculty appointments to members of one sex if a religious tenet of the controlling organization requires that faculty members be members of a religious order that admits one sex only. (2) Military schools are exempt if their *primary purpose* is to train individuals for the military services of the United States or the merchant marine. This exemption does not apply just because an institution may offer ROTC. (3) Private undergraduate institutions, traditionally and continually single-sex public undergraduate institutions, and elementary and secondary schools other than vocational schools are exempt from the *admissions* provisions of Title IX. Discrimination in admissions *is* prohibited in vocational institutions, all graduate and professional institutions, and public undergraduate coeducational institutions. *These exemptions apply to admissions only; they do not exempt institutions from the obligation to treat students equally once they are admitted to a program.*

Title IX of the Education Amendments Act is patterned after Title VI of the Civil Rights Act of 1964, which prohibits discrimination—on the basis of race, color, and national origin, but not sex—against the beneficiaries of programs receiving federal money. Like Title VI, Title IX is enforced by the Office for Civil Rights of the Department of Health, Education, and Welfare. It provides students with the legal justification to protest sex discrimination. It is a potentially powerful tool: if an institution does not comply with its provisions, the government may delay money, take back money previously awarded to the institution, or debar the institution from receiving future contracts or grants.

The following issues illustrate the kinds of problem areas that an institution concerned with providing its female students with an equal education must address. Many of these issues are also covered by existing legislation.

Sex-blind admissions. Although the law now requires that all public undergraduate coeducational institutions, all vocational institutions, all graduate and professional schools, and all institutions training individuals for the health professions admit students on the basis of their credentials rather than their reproductive organs, many women are asking not only that these provisions be enforced but that private undergraduate institutions drop their quotas on women. If an institution wants a student body of the highest caliber possible, why do quotas based on sex exist? The most often cited reason is that women are "bad risks." However, the career patterns of educated women do not confirm this assumption. A 1968 study showed that 91 percent of the women who received their doctorates in 1957 and 1958 were working. Of those who were working at the time of the survey, 79 percent had never interrupted their careers, and only 18 percent had experienced career interruption lasting from eleven to fifteen months (a figure roughly comparable to the interruption of men because of military service).[4]

Under Title IX of the Education Amendments Act of 1972, all coeducational public undergraduate and graduate institutions must have sex-blind admissions. That is, they cannot have a quota on either sex, and they cannot require higher standards for admis-

[4] Helen S. Astin, *The Woman Doctorate in America* (Hartford, Conn.: The Russell Sage Foundation, 1969), p. 58.

sion from one sex. However, changes in admissions policies and practices come slowly, even when the law mandates nondiscrimination. For example, some medical schools were reluctant to sign the government assurance (under the amendments to the Public Health Service Act) that they would admit women and men on an equal basis. Other institutions, even public institutions supported by the taxes of both women and men, often have quotas on women or require that women be more qualified to be admitted. For example, until the spring of 1973 the University of Georgia, like many other institutions (both public and private), had a 40 percent quota on women. Until the fall of 1972, according to a Stanford University press release, Stanford University had a 1933 regulation on the books which limited the enrollment of women to 40 percent.

Discrimination in admissions and the lack of encouragement women get to pursue their education are two of the primary reasons why women are underrepresented in higher education. In 1968, women made up 43 percent of those receiving bachelor's degrees and less than 13 percent of those awarded doctorates.[5] According to the National Manpower Council, only one of *three hundred women* in the United States today with the potential to earn a Ph.D. does so, while one of every thirty men with the potential receives a doctorate.[6]

Financial aid. The inability of women to compete equally with men for financial aid at many institutions tells women that their education is considered less important than the education of men. A study by the Educational Testing Service found that, although women and men need equal amounts of financial aid in college, the average award to a man was $215 higher than to a woman.[7] Another study, by Elizabeth W. Haven and Dwight H. Horsch,[8] found that undergraduate female applicants for financial

[5] U. S. Congress, House of Representatives, Committee on Education and Labor, Special Subcommittee on Education, *Discrimination Against Women*, "Statement of Peter Muirhead," June 16, 1970, p. 643.

[6] Harry G. Shaffer and Juliet P. Shaffer, "Job Discrimination Against Faculty Wives," Journal of Higher Education, XXXVI (January 1966), pp. 10–15.

[7] Birch Bayh, "Prohibition of Sex Discrimination," *Congressional Record*, February 28, 1972, p. S2746.

[8] *How Students Finance Their Education: A National Survey of the Educational Interests, Aspirations and Finances of College Sophomores in 1969–70* (New York: College Entrance Examination Board, January 1972);

aid were on the average better qualified than the male applicants, and their financial aid was equivalent, but that the women had greater difficulty in obtaining aid and had to rely more heavily on loans. Helen S. Astin[9] has reported a similar pattern at the graduate level. The women doctorates in her study were less likely to receive aid from the government or from their institutions and were therefore more likely to rely on their own savings or support from their families and/or spouses.

Faculty attitudes. The same assumptions that often lead financial-aid committees to give priority to male students often cause faculty to treat women differently in the classroom. Although the discouragement that women often receive from faculty may be benign in intent, it often has the effect of devastating career aspirations and feelings of self-worth in the embryonic stage. Often unwittingly, professors reinforce sex stereotypes. In a 1970 study of the status of women at the University of California at Berkeley, the women interviewed reported example after example of this type of discrimination:

> *Professors in the department generally took males more seriously—socialized with them, gave them special tasks.*

> *I was told, "I'd never accept a woman graduate student unless she was unmarriageable."*

> *I entered UC as a freshman and, upon my first interview with an advisor, was advised that it was silly for a woman to be serious about a career, that the most satisfying job for a woman is that of wife and mother.*[10]

A well-meaning faculty member who serves on the affirmative action committee at a Maryland community college distributed

---

abstract printed in 118 *Congressional Record* S2699 (daily ed., February 28, 1972).

[9] "Career Profiles of Women Doctorates," in Rossi Calderwood (Ed.), *Academic Women on the Move* (Hartford, Conn.: Russell Sage Foundation, 1973), pp. 8–32.

[10] Policy Committee of the Berkeley Division of the Academic Senate, *Report of the Subcommittee on the Status of Academic Women on the Berkeley Campus* (Berkeley: University of California, 1970), pp. 69–71.

the following notice to his spring semester students in 1973: "Unfortunately, most men write worse than I do, which is atrocious. For that reason, I prefer (strongly prefer) all such papers to be typed, solely for the purpose of legibility. *If you men cannot get such papers typed, please have your girl friend, wife, or mother write them for you* (emphasis added)."

It is hard to solve a problem unless there is recognition that a problem exists. Although the law now prohibits differential treatment of students on the basis of sex, those perpetuating the discrimination often do not even realize that they are in fact discriminating. All too often, sex discrimination or a sex-role stereotype is so widely accepted that it is regarded as the norm: a man being asked his grade-point average, a woman being asked her typing speed; a male science student being encouraged to go to medical school, while the woman who helped him pass organic chemistry is counseled to become a nurse or a laboratory technician; male science students being expected to build rockets, female science students being expected to wash test tubes; a woman athlete being regarded as a biological mistake, while a male athlete is admired as a "real man." All these assumptions—and many more like them—are widespread and deeply ingrained. At this point, only the faculty member with a keen sensitivity to women's concerns can free herself or himself from these limiting stereotypes.

Textbooks and curriculum. Textbooks from *Dick and Jane* to *Basic Anatomy* have come under fire for the biased, stereotyped portrayal of women. The Association of Women in Science (AWIS) forced publishers Williams and Wilkins to recall *The Anatomical Basis of Medical Practice* because of its portrayal of women. This text contained passages like these:

> *We are sorry that we cannot make available the addresses of the young ladies who grace our pages. Our wives burned our little address book at our last barbecue get-together.*

> *If you think that once you have seen the backside of one female, you have seen them all, then you haven't sat in a sidewalk cafe in Italy where girl watching is a cultivated*

art. Your authors, whose zeal in this regard never flags, refer
you to Figures III-50 and 53 as proof that female backs can
keep an interest in anatomy alive.

Thus the "little bit" of difference in a woman's built-
in biology urges her to ensnare a man. Such is the curse of
estrogen.

A new area of activity in higher education is the analysis of textbooks and documentation of omissions and stereotyping in them. For example, a study of twenty-seven college textbooks used in American history courses revealed the virtual absence of women: no book devoted more than 2 percent of its pages to women, and one devoted only .05 percent to women.

The number of women's studies courses has been increasing, and in the spring of 1973 there were well over a thousand. Although these courses are often excellent—rigorously academic as well as enlightening—they, much like black studies programs and continuing-education programs, often occupy only a fringe status at the college. Most people agree that women's studies courses are performing a vital role in educating women and men about the role of women in society. At the same time, however, they agree that the presence of a few women's studies courses does not relieve an institution from the obligation to take the sex bias out of *all* courses and materials. In short, women are beginning to use the principles established by the passage of Title IX, and the momentum for change, to encourage educational institutions and publishers to eliminate sex stereotyping in textbooks and materials, just as minorities used Title VI (of the Civil Rights Act of 1964) to force the elimination of racial and ethnic slurs and stereotypes.

Individual, unstereotyped counseling. Women are often discouraged from pursuing rigorous academic programs by well-intentioned counselors who urge them to train for traditionally female, dead-end, low-paying jobs rather than for traditionally male, upwardly mobile, high-paying, high-status jobs. In order to counsel women realistically for life in the twenty-first century, counselors need to become more familiar with the changing role of women in the marketplace and with the research on achievement and motivation in women. For example, counselors need to be more aware of what psychologist Matina Horner has called a woman's "motive to avoid success." Dr. Horner points out that it is this "fear of success" rather than a "desire to fail" which makes it especially difficult for women to excel either in school or in the world of work. Dr. Horner explains the dilemma in which women often find themselves: "Thus, consciously or unconsciously the girl equates intellectual achievement with a loss of femininity. A bright woman is caught in a double bind. In testing and other achievement-oriented situations, she worries not only about failure but also about success. If she fails, she is not living up to her own standards of performance; if she succeeds, she is not living up to societal expectations about the female role. Men in our society do not have this kind of ambivalence, because they are not only permitted but actively encouraged to do well."[11]

Not only do many counselors accept stereotyped notions about women and men; sometimes the very instruments used by counselors reflect similar notions. At its annual meeting in March 1972, the American Personnel and Guidance Association charged that the Strong Vocational Interest Blanks was discriminatory and called for its revision:

Whereas, the Strong Vocational Interest Blanks (SVIB) provide different occupational scores for men and women (that is, women cannot be scored on occupations like certified public accountant, purchasing agent, public administrator, and men cannot be scored on occupations such as medical technologist, recreation leader, physical education teacher); and whereas, when the same person takes both forms of the SVIB, the profiles turn out differently (for example, one woman scored high as a dental assistant, physical therapist, occupational therapist on the woman's profile, and physician, psychiatrist, and psychologist on the man's form); and whereas, the SVIB manual states: "Many young women do not appear to have strong occupational interests, and they may score high only in certain

---

[11] Matina Horner, "A Bright Woman Is Caught in a Double Bind," *Psychology Today*, 1969, *3*(6), 36–37.

'premarital' occupations: elementary school teacher, office worker, stenographer-secretary. Such a finding is disappointing to many college women, since they are likely to consider themselves career-oriented. In such cases, the selection of an area of training or an occupation should probably be based upon practical considerations, fields providing backgrounds that might be helpful to a wife and mother, occupations that can be pursued part time, are easily resumed after periods of nonemployment, and are readily available in different locales" (Campbell, rev. 1966, 13); therefore, be it resolved, that APGA commission duly authorize members to petition and negotiate with the SVIB publishers to revise their instruments, manuals, and norm groups so as to eliminate discrimination; and be it further resolved, that this duly authorized commission develop with the test publishers an explanatory paper to circulate among all purchasers of SVIB materials (including answer sheets) a statement which outlines the possible limitations inherent in the current SVIB with suggestions for ways to minimize the harm; and be it further resolved, that the commission on cooperation with the test publisher set a deadline for the new forms to be published and distributed.

Women students are asking for counselors, as well as instruments, that are sensitive to the changing roles of women; in some cases they are asking specifically for women counselors, claiming that male counselors are more likely to reinforce sex stereotypes.

Flexible programs. New approaches are needed to give the nontraditional student a fair chance in academe. Most college programs were designed for young males with few, if any, home or parental responsibilities. Institutions have often been slow to adapt their programs to students who do not fit into this model, such as older people returning to college or persons with parental responsibilities. Too often "flexibility" is interpreted as meaning "second rate," rather than an alternative way to achieve substantially the same results.

The lack of flexibility of a great many academic programs cannot help but make women anxious about how they can both marry and pursue their studies or a career. Although the trend is toward more equal sharing of work both in the home and in the labor force, most women still bear the principal responsibility for child rearing and housekeeping. Thus, they are less likely to be able to work or go to school full time, at least while their children are young.

The necessity of restrictive rules, such as on-campus residency requirements and time limits for degree completion, is being questioned. Also, some institutions, such as Westbrook College and Antioch College, offer credit for life experiences. Many of the nontraditional programs being developed will be helpful in breaking down the institutional barriers to educating many women.

Opportunities for older women. The same woman who can only attend school part-time might well be a woman who is not an 18- to 22-year-old "Betty Coed." Currently the woman who delayed her education so that she could raise a family often finds herself in a "damned-if-she-does, damned-if-she-doesn't" situation. Her children are in school, so the job of wife and mother may no longer be a satisfying full-time occupation. However, if she tries to go back to school, she is often told that she is too old for admission or past the cut-off age (often thirty-five) for eligibility for scholarship or fellowship aid.

Some institutions, such as those described in the case studies, are making unique efforts to help older women pursue an education. Other institutions often retain old roadblocks, despite the impressive body of knowledge that shows that older students are better academically and more highly motivated. We are all familiar with the veteran who was a mediocre high school student but who returns to graduate at the top of his college class. Paradoxically, women who have been out of school are not viewed in the same way. Yet a study by the Center for Continuing Education at Sarah Lawrence College[12] shows that women who return to college to earn undergraduate degrees demonstrate notably higher achievement and motivation than young undergraduates who complete their degrees in four years. According to the findings of this study, older women

[12] Melissa Lewis Richter and Jane Banks Whipple, *A Revolution in the Education of Women: Ten Years of Continuing Education at Sarah Lawrence College* (Bronxville: Sarah Lawrence College, 1972).

earn higher academic ratings, are less likely to drop out, and are more likely to continue into graduate school than their younger classmates.

Because fewer qualified women than men go to college or graduate school, older women returning to college make up the largest single group of potential new students. Many institutions are finding that one of the easiest ways to increase their lagging enrollment without diluting academic standards is to develop programs and services which facilitate the reentry of these women into academia.

Continuing-education programs, however excellent they may be, are not enough. Too often these programs are isolated from the mainstream of the university community, with small budgets which are the first to be cut in a financial squeeze, with a staff that has little stature in the university hierarchy, with untenured faculty, and with courses that are not transferable to regular degree programs. Where continuing-education programs have survived, they have indeed helped a number of individual women, and have often made significant contributions to innovation in higher education. Ideally, the strengths of these programs will be integrated into the overall university structure.

Equality in health and medical services. Although women make up about 40 percent of the college students, a survey by the National Student Association reveals that 53 percent of the college and university health services do not provide gynecological services, and fully 72 percent do not prescribe birth control for women.[13] On many campuses student health fees are used to pay team doctors for male sports but not to hire a gynecologist to meet the health needs of women. In fact, the health services of many institutions are of no help to a woman who needs gynecological care, treatment for venereal disease, or contraceptive advice. The lack of adequate medical services for women has become a central issue on some campuses. Students have staged sit-ins or demonstrations specifically protesting the inadequacy of the health-care facilities available to women on several campuses. Women on campus have cited some specific practices which they feel emphasize their second-class posi-

[13] Ann Scott, "How to Make Trouble: It's Time for Equal Education," *Ms.*, 1972, *1*(4), 122.

tion: inadequate services or facilities to meet the routine gynecological needs of women (atlhough the institution may provide urological services for males); lack of contraceptive information and services; treatment of pregnancy as different from any other temporary disability (although the principle of treating childbearing like any other medical disability is firmly established in the area of employment); limited insurance coverage for women (for example; policies that cover childbirth only for married women, policies that cover vasectomies but not sterilization, policies that cover pregnancy for faculty wives but not female employees, and policies that do not cover pregnancy at all; all of these policies tell a woman that her health—and, by inference, she herself—is not as important as the health of a male student or the health of the wife of a male employee).

Sports and athletic opportunities. The time, energy, and money spent on athletic opportunities and facilities for men but not women are coming under increasing criticism. Although there are some honest disagreements over what constitutes equality in sports and athletics, there is no question that—whatever the definition—in virtually every coeducational institution in the country women do not receive an equal opportunity in this area.

The inequities in money alone are tremendous. For example, women at a Big Ten university had to have bake sales and sell Christmas trees in order to finance their athletic activities. At one state university with an annual budget of approximately $800,000 for the male athletic teams, the women had difficulty getting $15,000 to finance their athletic activities.

The Women's Equity Action League (WEAL) has issued the following statement on athletic opportunities for women: "efforts to bring about equal opportunity [in athletics] for women must be twofold: While outstanding female athletes should not be excluded from competition because their schools provide teams only for males, separate but equal programs should also be provided for average female students, who cannot compete equally in athletics with male students."

The issues go beyond what to do about coeducational teams (or, to put it another way, that go beyond the question of whether or not a woman can play on the football team). A variety of questions are being asked and the legal clout of Title IX (of the Education Amendments Act of 1972) mandates that substantive answers be given to these questions: Why do the female teams and physical education departments generally have second-rate equipment and facilities? Why are the team and intramural opportunities for women generally less than those for men? Why are the coaches of female teams often paid less than their male counterparts? Why does the budget for female sports often come from the student government or from club fees, while the budget for male sports is often a separate item in the university budget? Why does the university provide transportation for the male, but not the female, teams? Why are some courses (such as coaching or instruction for some sports) open only to men? Why are female reporters sometimes barred from the press box? Why does the university health service often provide extensive medical assistance to the male, but not the female, teams?

Equalization of rules and regulations. A variety of rules and regulations—from curfew hours, to parietal hours, to dress codes, to requirements that women (but not men) live in on-campus housing—are being reviewed and challenged on campuses across the country. Increasingly, women and men are saying that these rules perpetuate the double standard and subtly tell women students that they are sexual objects who must be protected from themselves and from men.

Housing rules have sometimes been used in the past to deny women admission to an institution. For example, institutions assign a smaller number of rooms to women, then insist that all women live on campus, although male students are allowed to live anywhere they choose. The institution then claims that a shortage of dormitory rooms is the reason for limiting the admission of women.

Different rules on the basis of sex are now prohibited by Title IX of the Educational Amendments Act of 1972.

Women as student leaders. Other, more subtle factors which tend to limit female students are also at work. For example, often the percentage of female student leaders is as small as the percentage of tenured women full professors. We can assume that the effect is similar as well; that is, if women students see few women in responsible positions, they are less likely to aspire to those positions themselves, no matter how qualified they are. Some institutions are making a conscious effort to increase the number of women in leadership positions by appointing them to committees. However, the presence of a disproportionate number of men in student leadership positions—president of the student body, editor of the newspaper or literary magazine, president of other organizations and groups—raises some serious questions about the message that the institution is conveying to women students.

Equal job opportunities. Some institutions are now specifically including a section on student employment in their affirmative-action plans. Discrimination in student employment (including work-study programs) is prohibited by the same laws and regulations that prohibit discrimination on the basis of sex among regular employees: Executive Order 11246, Title VII of the Civil Rights Act of 1964, the Equal Pay Act of 1963, and Title IX of the Education Amendments Act of 1972. These laws prohibit any differences on the basis of sex in hiring, upgrading, salaries, fringe benefits, training, and all other conditions of employment. Practices such as routinely assigning female students to secretarial jobs and male students to the higher-paying grounds and buildings crew are in violation of these laws. Another example of discrimination against student employees: A woman at a coeducational ivy league institution who applied for a job in the university greenhouse was told that girls were not hired to work there because "they kill the plants."

Student placement services which accept job opportunities limited to one sex are in violation of the law themselves and (in all probability) are assisting the employer in violating the law. However benign the intent, this breakdown virtually always limits the job opportunities of women students. For example, relatively low-paying jobs (such as secretarial work and teaching) are listed for women, while the better jobs (such as engineering and middle-management positions) are listed for men. This sort of categorization is almost identical to sex-segregated help-wanted advertisements (which are in violation of the *Guidelines on Discrimination Because of Sex* of Title VII of the Civil Rights Act of 1964).

Some women also find it more difficult than their male counterparts to get substantial recommendations for graduate school or employment from their professors. Ruth C. Benson, formerly director of Equal Opportunity at the University of Maine, summarizes some of these problems: "Evaluations of their [women's] intellect and professional promise are all but lost in comments on their looks and their potential as 'castrating females' or 'cuddly bunnies.' (I'm quoting from actual letters of reference.)"[14]

Coeducation versus single-sex institutions. There are many arguments both for and against coeducation. Perhaps the strongest argument for a women's college is that the women's colleges, not the coeducational colleges, are actively concerned with developing new and more effective ways to educate women. This concern is reflected in the achievement of women students after graduation. Elizabeth Tidball[15] has found that a disproportionately high number of successful career women are graduates of women's colleges. At coeducational colleges women often are admitted only as an afterthought and, once admitted, are offered only second-class citizenship.

The faculty, the administration, and the student leadership of most coeducational institutions are, in all probability, composed mostly of males. For that matter, the faculty and the administration of a good many female institutions also are composed mostly of males. Perhaps it is a misnomer to call institutions "female" on the basis of the composition of their student body; perhaps it would be more accurate to define institutions by the composition of their power structures.

There is no unilateral answer to the issue of "which is best" for women, a women's college or a coeducational institution. At this point, however, some women's colleges, but practically no coeducational institutions, are actively concerned with the education of women.

Visibility of women in campus publications. Promotional, recruiting, or other materials often unintentionally tell women that they are either invisible or viewed primarily as dates or sex objects. Overuse of the word *he* is one subtle way of excluding women. Other exclusions are not so subtle. For example, in the catalog of one of the most prestigious scientific schools in the country, women

---

[14] Speech given at the 55th annual meeting of the American Council on Education, October 6, 1972.
[15] "Perspectives on Women" (see footnote 2).

are conspicuously absent from the pictures and the few women pictured are clearly "dates."

Compensatory activities. As a sign of their concern for their female students, some institutions have undertaken remedial activities, activities designed to eliminate institutional discrimination against women. For example, commissions on the status of women have been formed on some campuses to deal with discrimination against female students and employees. At least forty campuses have women's centers, groups specifically designed to be responsive to the needs of women. Also, some institutions, such as Tufts University, have undertaken studies of the status of women students on their campus to identify specific problem areas so that they can plan for the future.

All these factors—the presence of female role models, the services provided for women, the attitudes of faculty and counselors, and the other issues discussed on the preceding pages—tell a woman a great deal more about an institution than any college catalog can. Together these factors create the total learning climate for women. If the environment is not positive, if the synthesis of these factors tells women that they are not very important to the university, then it is highly unlikely that the needs of either society or the women on campus will be met. If, however, this climate is positive, if the institution is truly concerned with the education of women, then it will inevitably develop programs to enable women to assume their fair place in society.

♪ 4 ♪

Minority Groups

*B*oth the presence and the influence of Blacks and other minorities in American higher education have increased substantially in recent years. In the fall of 1970, according to the best available estimates, the combined minority enrollment was about 10 percent of the total, and by almost any interpretation that represents a significant growth. Beyond numbers, the influence of nonwhites in higher education has resulted in some far-reaching institutional changes in such areas as access, retention, curriculum, and public service. Nevertheless, American higher education remains overwhelmingly white, both in its complexion and in its collective attitude, and minor adjustments have been far more common than fundamental changes. Institutional attempts to depart from the established patterns of meritocracy and white privilege may have a subtle influence, but they almost never result in dramatic new directions. Homogenization seems to continue unchecked in spite of occasional departures from the path or the pace.

American higher education's record of service to Blacks and other minorities, then, is not impressive. The nation's Black colleges and universities have struggled for a century against systematic segregation and discrimination, and their accomplishments have usually come in spite of the rest of higher education, not because of it. Indians and Chicanos in particular are the forgotten people. For many Chicanos and Indians, education itself has often been a travesty, and higher education a total impossibility. Relatively few in number, isolated geographically, and only recently verging on militancy, they are just beginning to break out of the schools that deny both their traditions and their future, and to establish institutions of their own.

Although the different minority groups have their own special concerns and problems, they have in common a need for better higher-education opportunities than they have heretofore received in a primarily Anglo society. This chapter illustrates some efforts being made in that direction. The first two schools discussed, Malcolm-King Harlem College and Nairobi College, are examples of the new enterprises that have been started as "alternative" institutions for Blacks. DQU represents a joint venture by Indians and Chicanos, a free-wheeling attempt to start an entirely new school on an abandoned army base outside Davis, California. Navajo College is an all-Indian college, the only college established on a reservation at the time this report was written.

Finally, Pima College and Third College illustrate noteworthy and promising attempts at pluralism—attempts to build an institution around the principle of multiracial, multiethnic, multicultural parity. Pima College in particular is seeking to prove that respect for and appreciation of differences among peoples can be woven into the fabric of a university; that the trend toward homogeneity in our institutions can be checked by a concerted effort to preserve diversity; and that it is possible to have national unity without threatening racial and cultural and ethnic identity.

Malcolm-King Harlem College Extension

John Egerton

Harlem's first institution of higher learning could be characterized as an unconventional attempt to provide the conventional rewards of a college education to a group of people who previously have been denied that opportunity. It is a no-cost night college offering mostly liberal-arts courses to a student body made up primarily of working adults.

Mattie Cook, a Harlem resident and a former Head Start director, conceived the idea for the college with a small group of community workers in the fall of 1967. Together with a local parish priest, representatives of an interfaith alliance, a nun from Marymount Manhattan College, and two members of the Intermediate School 201 governing board, Mrs. Cook launched the experiment by offering a course in theater arts to thirteen students in the spring of 1968. The following fall three courses were offered, and the College of Mount Saint Vincent joined in the project. A year later the curriculum was expanded to nineteen courses, and Fordham University became the third institution to affiliate with the venture. In the fall of 1972 almost six hundred students were enrolled in about sixty-five courses.

Malcolm-King College prides itself on its community origins. Mrs. Cook and three other persons, who devoted countless hours to the project, received no pay (they held full-time jobs elsewhere), and all of its faculty were volunteers from the three participating colleges and from the Harlem area. Its classes were held in three centers made available by local institutions. Says Mrs. Cook: "The college began from a feeling of community concern. We had people with ability and skills but no paper credentials. Only 2 percent of the population in this area has had any college education. We need leaders. We had to have classes in the community after working hours. We couldn't charge tuition. We had to have a faculty which included skilled Blacks. And all we could contribute was some space to hold classes in. So we went looking for help, and we found it."

In 1970 Malcolm-King received a $75,000 grant from the Student Special Services branch of the United States Office of Education and $43,000 from the New York State Department of Education's Higher Educational Opportunity Program. With the funds, a full-time administrative staff was able to solidify the college's structure and give it more of an appearance of permanence. In 1971, for the first time, a registration fee of five dollars a semester was requested of all students able to pay it. But all of the institution's seventy-two faculty members still volunteered their services in

1972–1973, and classes were still held in the same three donated community locations (a public school, a Catholic school, and a community office complex).

Marymount Manhattan, Mount St. Vincent, and Fordham have formalized their relationship with Malcolm-King by making the college an official extension of themselves. Most of the Harlem institution's faculty come from the three schools, and their presidents and academic deans serve on Malcolm-King's administrative council. Furthermore, students can transfer up to sixty credits—two full years of study—to any of the three institutions, and a similar transfer privilege has now been negotiated with the City University of New York.

Mrs. Cook is Malcolm-King's administrative director. She and her staff of about twenty-five persons, which includes several of the college's students, have an office on the eleventh floor of a Harlem office building at 103 East 125th Street. As the school has grown and knowledge of its presence has spread, in Harlem as well as elsewhere, the administrative work load has multiplied. Correspondence, record keeping, counseling, committee work, and liaison with the affiliated institutions all have increased. And Mrs. Cook adds: "We're seen as a program of merit in the community now, and we're being asked to take on some new assignments, such as drug-abuse education and courses for day-care-center workers."

Malcolm-King offers two different kinds of community-service programs, in addition to its regular courses. The first includes a training and certificate program in cooperation with CHAMP (Central Harlem Association of Montessori Parents); a job-training program for workers in the drug rehabilitation field, in cooperation with Skills Advancement, Inc., and the Harlem Hospital's Department of Community Health; a program in early-childhood education for several local day-care centers; and a course on critical issues in education, in conjunction with the Harlem Parents' Union. The second type of community-service program involves vocational training for individuals not affiliated with a cooperating institution. Included in this category are a program in counseling, to help local ministers deal with social problems in their community and personal problems in their congregations; a training course for people interested in computer programming; and a series of education courses to improve the skills of teacher aides.

The Malcolm-King curriculum looks something like the curriculum of a liberal-arts junior college. Courses include English and Spanish, composition and speech, literature and drama, history and sociology, politics and government, teacher education, pre-law, economics, mathematics, and psychology. If the curriculum seems fairly standard, the student body is not. It is made up principally of working adults. Most of them are Black, but there are a few Puerto Ricans, whites, and others. Most of the students are women —mothers and grandmothers. The only entrance requirement is a high school diploma or an equivalency certificate, and that rule is sometimes bent to admit people who are in the process of completing high school work. A three-credit course meets for two and a half hours one night a week, and since classes are held Tuesday through Thursday, it is possible for a student to enroll for nine hours of credit each sixteen-week semester. In the summer of 1971 fifteen women students graduated in the college's first commencement, and most of them are continuing—some with scholarships— in one of the baccalaureate degree programs of the cooperating colleges. Mrs. Cook says that the college is recruiting younger students—recent high school graduates—and more males.

The students are active in all aspects of the program. In addition to those employed on the administrative staff, there is a student government, a number of committees managing student interests, and student involvement in such basic and important matters as curriculum selection and faculty evaluation. Further, the current chairman of the college's administrative council—the equivalent of a board of directors—is also a student. And it was the students who chose the college's name.

Most of the students come from the Harlem and East Harlem communities, but some Bronx and Brooklyn residents also are enrolled. Virtually all of them have jobs, but most are low-paid employees classified as "unskilled." The college, recognizing their special needs, is trying to find ways to give them support through such services as babysitting for their small children, tutoring and remedial instruction for themselves, and a textbook lending and purchasing system. Cooperating colleges and the city library provide needed library and study facilities, although the arrangements are not entirely satisfactory. A study-skills center in the college office also is providing help to students who need it.

One of Malcolm-King's top priorities is to get more Black males involved in the program. At the student level some thought has been given to establishing a male quota. At the faculty level some progress has been made in moving from a predominantly white, female, religious group to one that in 1972–1973 was about 50 percent Black. About half of the faculty either have doctorates or are doctoral candidates. Most of the Blacks who teach lack those credentials but have special skills and experience which make them especially valuable. Some began teaching at Malcolm-King as interns, supervised in a team-teaching arrangement under the direction of a regular professor, and then moved to solo teaching. Some have been made adjunct professors at Marymount, St. Vincent, and Fordham.

Considering the relatively small investment that has been made in Malcolm-King College, the returns from it are remarkable. It is providing an opportunity in higher education for about six hundred students each semester—students who would not otherwise be in college. It is becoming an effective and productive institution of higher education in a vast, densely populated area that does not even have a public high school, let alone a college. It has drawn three Catholic colleges into a useful role of public service. And perhaps most important of all, it is demonstrating a significant truth that American higher education often seems to have lost sight of: that every college does not need to be a Harvard. With flexibility, with ingenuity, with improvisation, and just a little bit of money, Malcolm-King has been successful enough already to justify its existence. It is preparing people to enter into the competitive race for credentials in a meritocratic society, but in doing so it is also raising some timely questions about the whole credentialing process. "The objective should be broadening knowledge, not getting credentials," says Mrs. Cook, who is an M.A. graduate of Columbia's Teachers College.

However promising Malcolm-King's approach may appear to be, however, it faces some difficult problems, some of which are created by the meritocratic system itself. For 1972–1973 it has received a total of $186,000 in federal and state aid, an increase of $34,000 over last year, but those funds will dry up at some point unless the college becomes accredited. The City University of New York has shown some interest in making Malcolm-King a junior college within its system, but that would mean giving up much of the flexibility that has allowed the school to stay afloat. More rigid requirements would be placed on the faculty, for example, and admission and enrollment could also be affected.

There appear to be four possible routes open to Malcolm-King in the future. It could, first of all, move closer to any one of the cooperating colleges it is now affiliated with—or to all three of them—and become a full-fledged branch campus having equal status in all respects. That seems unlikely, though, because of the costs involved; the private colleges are already strapped for funds, and their financial status does not seem likely to improve anytime soon.

Second, Malcolm-King could join the City University system. Mrs. Cook is skeptical of that choice for several reasons beyond the ones already mentioned. "We would have to expand too much, too quickly," she says. "I'm afraid the emphasis would be on quantity rather than quality. And there are other problems. They want just recent high school graduates, not older students like so many of ours are. Costs would also be a barrier, and so would accessibility. CUNY is now supposedly an open-enrollment institution, but that means high school graduates with academic diplomas, whereas we will take any kind of high school diploma. There is informal discouragement of students with unimpressive credentials at many of the CUNY colleges, and there is also a high dropout rate. We don't discourage anybody from entering, but we don't lose many, either."

A third possibility for the college is linkage with the State University of New York system, and Mrs. Cook thinks that route might offer more promise. It is, at this point, an option that has not been fully explored.

The fourth choice is complete independence. It would be the most difficult of all, though probably the most satisfying to the students and the community, if it could be accomplished. The principal obstacles appear to be money and accreditation. Mrs. Cook is inquiring about accreditation with officials of the regional agency that handles such matters. The money problem, though, seems almost insurmountable for the long run. With a small student body, a volunteer faculty, and donated space, the college has been highly successful. But growth is inevitable, and it is doubtful whether it can be sustained on a volunteer basis.

Mrs. Cook, an energetic and self-assured woman, is not dismayed by the hard choices facing her college. She talks confidently of being able to offer the Associate of Arts degree, and perhaps even the Bachelor of Arts—either as an independent college or as a separate campus in a larger system.

Whatever course Malcolm-King follows, it has already proved its worth. It has brought higher education to Harlem and made it work for people, and the people who have been involved in it are evidence that the approach is effective.

There is, of course, no bank of standardized test data available to measure the aptitude or achievement of Malcolm-King students. In one sense the college can be viewed as a sort of case in point against overreliance on such tests, or against uncritical belief in their infallibility. The ultimate measure of Malcolm-King's effectiveness will derive from the performance of its students in the upper-division colleges to which they transfer, and the subsequent uses they are able to make of their formal education.

Malcolm-King is short on ideology—or, at least, short on rhetoric—and long on pragmatism. Its clientele are people who have been victimized by "the system," by racism and class prejudice, and its objective is to teach them how to negotiate that system, how to make it work for them. That is, in a way, a nonrevolutionary ideal, one with ample historical precedent. But it is also a challenge to the system of American higher education. Malcolm-King is trying to prove that people who want to learn and people who want to teach will always make a winning combination, no matter what test scores or past performances say about it. It has brought such a combination together: professors whose desire to teach transcends considerations of money, convenience, and prestige, and students whose desire to learn is obviously very great. Not many colleges are blessed with such a combination. If, because of experimental ventures such as Malcolm-King, America's higher education system should be moved to change, the revolutionary potential might prove to be greater than it appears on the surface.

♪ Nairobi College ♪

John Egerton

For almost a decade frustration over the manifold deficiencies of American higher education has been spawning new attempts to change the structure. Free universities, storefront colleges, and alternative schools have blossomed all across the landscape. Most of them have faded as fast as they bloomed. Nairobi College, which began its third year in 1971, is a notable exception. It has not yet become all that its statement of purpose (quoted below) envisions, but it may well have moved farther along that road than any other recent venture of its type.

"The cities and colleges of this country are in disrepair. Many of those who would rebuild them would tear them down first. Nairobi College is an alternative to tearing down. It is an alternative to an educational system which serves many people badly and people of color not at all.

"Nairobi College comes out of the unmet needs of peoples of color for education but is open to all students who find it a viable educational alternative. It will not level buildings which are still functional to create a walled-off fortress of hallowed learning; it will not destroy a student's culture to replace it with one that fits him badly; it will not separate generation from generation or race from race so that one may climb on the shaky foundation of the ruins of the other; it will not strip students of their dignity or their ability to determine their own destinies, forcing them to follow a leadership they neither understand nor respect; it will not consider itself above the analysis of its product by those it seeks to serve.

"Nairobi College is being designed to produce what communities of color need: doctors, lawyers, engineers, skilled businessmen, capable technicians, and able public officials and social scientists who are a part of the community that they intend to serve and who serve the community while they develop their expertise.

"Nairobi College is being designed with the belief that colleges can be built without walls, that they can be . . . a part of the communities they serve. It is being designed with the belief that colleges can be governed by the communities, the students, and the faculty they serve, that they can bridge the gap between knowledge and action by being institutions which initiate and participate in the activities of the communities building themselves and their peoples. It is designed with the belief that the college and its students serve the community and are evaluated by the community. Nairobi College is designed with the belief that no one need destroy his past or strip himself of his dignity to become a liberated human being."

The word *alternative* seems naturally to belong in the description of Nairobi. In its makeup as well as in its philosophy, it is a Black institution, and thus an alternative to white-dominated colleges and universities. As a separate, independent, and un-affiliated school, it operates outside the system of established institutions, public and private. And because it is, to quote its statement of purpose, "an alternative to tearing down," it has set for itself the formidable task of proving that destruction and anarchy are not necessary prerequisites to revolutionary change.

Since it opened in 1969, Nairobi has changed rapidly in several ways, but its basic objective is the same: to develop Black leadership in and for a Black community. Its intent is to provide two years of academic training and a whole lifetime of psychological reeducation for Black citizens of East Palo Alto, California, a low-income community separated by a freeway from its opulent neighbors in San Mateo County, south of San Francisco. East Palo Alto is an unincorporated community of about 25,000 people, over 80 percent of them Black. It is not an urban slum, in the way that sections of Chicago or Newark are, and its people are not poor like the rural poor of Mississippi; it is simply a neglected and under-developed appendage of one of the nation's richest counties. The contrast is visible and stark.

One of East Palo Alto's citizens is Robert Hoover, a thirty-nine-year-old North Carolinian who went west in the late 1950s to do graduate work at San Jose State College and Stanford University (Stanford is barely two miles away, across the freeway) and for awhile was involved in a program for minority students at the College of San Mateo, a junior college in the California network

of two-year institutions. The latter experience was punctuated by
turbulence and conflict, and Hoover came out of it determined to
provide Black students with another option. "When I was at the
College of San Mateo," he recalls, "I used to say the purpose of
our program was to train leaders to build Black communities. The
college people always insisted that wasn't the college's job, but I
said, 'Why not? You do it for white people all the time.' " Hoover
was convinced that the college was both unwilling and unable to
meet the basic academic and psychological needs of Black and
Chicano students, and Nairobi College came into being as a result
of that conviction.

    With $80,000 raised from private sources, Hoover and a
handful of colleagues—mostly Blacks, but including some whites and
Chicanos—opened the school in 1969 in a house in East Palo Alto.
They had over one hundred students in classes scattered throughout
the community and a volunteer faculty drawn from neighboring
institutions and from nonacademic sources. No one—including
Hoover, the college's first president—drew a salary; the budget was
used for rent, utilities, supplies, books, and student aid. The curriculum was a mixture of routine and radical: English, Swahili,
mathematics, leadership development, Black psychology, political
awareness. Students over eighteen were admitted without regard to
their prior academic record, and they were involved fully in decision
making and administration, including faculty and student selection,
curriculum development, and fiscal matters. Community involvement was also a integral part of the structure: students were given
work-study assignments in East Palo Alto, and local citizens participated in governance of the college.

    Several white people were engaged in administrative work,
a number of others taught courses, and three whites were in the
student body. There were also from the beginning some important,
if informal, ties with various departments at Stanford. But Nairobi's
ideological orientation was distinctly nonwhite. It was a third-world
college, for "people of color"—black, brown, red, and yellow. It
originally had plans for developing additional campuses in Redwood City, Daly City, South San Francisco, San Francisco's China-
town, and Alcatraz—all communities where there are concentrations
of Chicanos, Indians, Chinese, or other nonwhites.

    As an inevitable consequence of the collective experiences

of Nairobi's nonwhite majority—and as a reflection of the temper of the times—antiwhite sentiment was strong. As time passed, most of the whites who were connected with the college either dropped out or were pushed out. But in spite of these tensions, Nairobi never got caught in ideological quicksand, thanks largely to the maturity and equilibrium of the organizers. There was Black rage and hostility and talk of total estrangement from whites, but Hoover and his colleagues kept the energy focused on building an institution to serve the community, and they managed to keep the college on the course without either separating from or surrendering to outside forces.

There were no white people visibly involved in Nairobi in 1971; yet the college seems to have moved beyond any preoccupation with rhetoric to a more pragmatic stage. Original plans to develop other campuses have not materialized, except that the Chicanos who were once a part of Nairobi have parted company to run their own enterprise—Venceremos College—in nearby Redwood City. Hoover says simply, "We weren't ready for it. The leadership of the two communities was not together. Coalitions between people of color are still important, but the problems are not going to be solved anytime soon. Meanwhile, we have to remember that our first priority is to build this community."

Hoover's perception of Black nationalism finds expression in community building. He makes a clear distinction between the nuts-and-bolts work of developing self-sufficient communities and the theoretical abstractions of nation-building in the grand design. It is not that Black nationalism or pan-Africanism or third-world nation-building are concepts of no interest to him; it is rather that East Palo Alto is a sort of practical application of those ideologies, and he is more interested in the application—in economic, political, social, and educational self-determination—than in the theory. He and the other molders of Nairobi have kept themselves occupied with their college, their town, its population, its problems, and its relationship to the rest of San Mateo County. They want to see Nairobi produce young people who are academically and psychologically prepared to move into other institutions for further training and then come back to contribute to East Palo Alto's development. That has been its basic mission and its primary objective from the first.

In 1971 Nairobi had about three hundred students, still

scattered in classrooms throughout the community, and offered more than sixty courses between the hours of 8 A.M. and 9 P.M. five days a week. For the most part, it was a meat-and-potatoes curriculum—business administration, music, English, French, Swahili, African and Afro-American literature, education, mathematics, physics, biology, and a good selection of social science courses, including several which focus on Black interest. There were nine full-time faculty members, nine full-time staff members (several of whom also teach a course or two), and about a dozen volunteer faculty members who teach part time. Nairobi operated on a budget of approximately $285,000 in 1971–1972. About 60 percent of this came from federal grants and loans—Work-Study, EOG, NDSL, Talent Search, and Student Special Services. The rest came from private donations.

Donald Smothers, a twenty-six-year-old East Palo Alto resident, serves as president, and Robert Hoover is director of academic affairs, a position which frees him from much of the day-to-day administrative responsibility so that he can teach two courses (in education and political awareness) and spend more time on community involvements and long-range planning for the college. Smothers, a graduate of San Francisco State College, is one of eight Nairobi faculty and staff members who once were enrolled in the minority-student program that Hoover ran at the College of San Mateo.

Nairobi enrolls slightly more men than women students, and the average age of the student body is about twenty-five—an indication that middle-aged people as well as young adults are attending. There are still no entrance requirements. The college charges its students $600 a year, but financial aid—including all costs, even books and supplies—is provided, and about 95 percent of the students get some form of assistance. All the students are Black, and a substantial minority of them now come from outside East Palo Alto, including six from Africa. The college has aspirations of building formal ties with some African countries and stimulating a two-way flow of students and faculty. Closer to home, Nairobi still maintains working relationships with several departments at Stanford for various kinds of technical assistance, and in 1971–1972 about a dozen Nairobi graduates transferred to junior-year degree programs at Stanford, the University of California at Berkeley, and the California State Universities at San Jose and Hayward.

Although Nairobi's curriculum, class structure, and calendar (quarter system) tend to follow traditional patterns, some interesting new wrinkles have been added. Grades, for example, are A-B-C, but nothing is recorded for those who do not earn a passing grade, and students can repeat courses as many times as necessary to get a better grade. A sort of buddy system is utilized to match students on a one-and-one basis for tutoring, and Friday afternoons are set aside for this activity. On Friday mornings all faculty and staff, as well as many students, are engaged in a wide-ranging convocation that deals with social, political, organizational, and community matters. Between quarters the college community goes on a retreat, where past performance is reviewed and plans are made for the next term of school. And in all of this, the student input is substantial.

The most unusual and impressive characteristics of Nairobi are not in the academic realm, though, important as that is to the students. Most significant—and most worthy of replication elsewhere—are the ways in which the college has made itself a vital part of the community it serves. Its governing board, for example, is made up of three students, three faculty and staff members, and three community residents, chosen by their peers. The main office of the college is located in a shopping center, and negotiations are underway to rent an empty supermarket there and convert it to classroom and office use. A fully licensed child-care center is operated for children of students and staff, free of charge. Several inmates from the Vacaville State Prison have been released to the college; three of them teach, and two others serve as staff members organizing a tutoring and counseling program for Vacaville inmates. The college's talent-search program, called Dig It, recruits high school students and college dropouts and serves as their broker for reentry into higher education at Nairobi or other schools.

Still other kinds of community service are evident. Nairobi is leading a community fight against drug pushers, and against the attending theft problems often found where drug traffic is heavy. Student counseling has become community counseling, not only for educational matters but also for juveniles in trouble with the law, for welfare mothers, and for others with pressing social needs. The school library, with 20,000 volumes collected by students in a county book drive, has potential as a community resource. Nairobi is not just a college; it is a community-service agency in a community where service is extremely scarce. In many ways it is an institutional ombudsman for citizens of East Palo Alto.

The college has a counterpart alternative institution at the elementary and secondary school level in the Nairobi Day School, begun in 1966 by Gertrude Wilks, a local resident and an exceptional woman in her own right. There is no official connection between the two institutions, but Bob Hoover was the first principal of the day school, and he serves on its board. Hoover is also an elected member of the board of the Ravenswood School District, which encompasses East Palo Alto and the adjoining area. The district has 5500 students, 85 percent of them Black, in eleven schools, seven of which are in East Palo Alto's Black community. Two of the five board members are Black, and Hoover calls it "a pretty good board." He adds: "In the past few years we've had some real change. Before, there were only twenty Black teachers out of 350, one Black man in the central office, and one Black principal. Now we have a Black superintendent, ninety Black teachers, and half of the principals and vice-principals are Black. And the quality of education has gone up—the average youngster in the first three grades is reading above grade level, and we never had that before." If such changes continue, there may no longer be a need for the Nairobi Day School—in which case it will have played a pivotal role as an alternative institution.

Hoover and his colleagues in the college see no such possibility for them. "There is no way we could become a part of the College of San Mateo," he says flatly. "We'd rather close than go the state school route." The reasons are not hard to see. While it is conceivable that the local public school system could become effective enough to obviate the need for Nairobi Day School, it is hard to imagine the College of San Mateo's accommodating itself to the kind of activist role Nairobi College is playing. Nairobi's concerns are focused on East Palo Alto, where fewer than one tenth of San Mateo County's residents live. East Palo Alto is not only unincorporated; it is also without a resident representative on the county's nine-member, all-white governing board, and it is policed by the county sheriff's department, which is also overwhelmingly white. These matters are a preoccupation with the people of East Palo Alto, including those at Nairobi College, and they draw a direct correlation between the makeup of county government and the laxness of government services in their community. To people like Bob Hoover, that is not an abstract problem to be viewed with academic detachment; it is something to be met head on. The college does just that, aggressively and persistently. It is, in a sense, a political force, pushing for such things as an adequate drainage system and more effective police protection. It wants to get federal funds to build two hundred units of low-cost public housing. And it is probably the leading advocate of East Palo Alto's incorporation as a separate municipality.

Not many colleges do things like that, and it can be convincingly argued that in ordinary circumstances such activities are not proper functions for an academic institution. But East Palo Alto's circumstances are not ordinary, and Nairobi is something more than just a college. It is in the business of community building, training Black people to be leaders in a Black community suffering from the ill effects of racism and absentee government. "A separate Black country inside this country is not a real option," says Hoover, "but Black communities are—they are a reality. This is one of them. So our objectives are the same as they always were: We're trying to rescue people, to give them direction, to bring back skills and expertise to our community. All the rhetoric about revolution, about change—it's no good if you don't know what you're after, and if a lot of talk is all you've got you're not going anywhere."

Nairobi can see its way ahead for about three more years, but the long-range prospects are not favorable for such a risky venture. Obstacles are everywhere. There is, for instance, the matter of funding, a perennial problem now for even the most secure institutions. "Unless the independent Black schools can come together and raise funds from Black communities," Hoover says, "we can't survive." And there is the problem of multiple purposes, of mixing education and politics and ideology and activism. It has been tried before, and the track record is very poor.

Somehow, though, a bet on Nairobi doesn't seem like wasting money. The school has reached "candidate" status in its progression toward accreditation, and a visiting team from the Western Association of Schools and Colleges concluded in 1971 that "Nairobi College is well conceived and psychologically planned to meet its educational objectives in an effective manner. . . . The college is highly creative in utilizing the initiative and motivation of students, faculty, and community to build a strong sense of belonging or family-oriented concept of concern for the college and the community in which it is located and which it serves."

But accreditation is hardly a guarantee of survival, says Hoover: "Our chances of staying alive are very slim, there's no question about it. I think we have about three years to find a mechanism for continued funding. If we haven't got it together by then, we won't make it. But I'm not sweating it. If we can get sixty to one hundred young people ready by then, with all the skills and the training they need, this community will have a priceless asset, and it'll be in good shape whether Nairobi survives or not."

There is no doubt that Nairobi College arouses mixed emotions at best, and fearful hostility at worst, among many white educators, not to mention many white citizens and government officials of San Mateo County. They see an institution apparently intent on breaking all the rules of pedagogy, protocol, and politics that the academic world has painstakingly put together over many long decades, and they seem to hear an antiwhite ideology emanating from an all-Black campus, and all of that must be very disquieting.

Yet after all the reservations about official activism and radical emphasis and antimeritocracy have been registered, the basic form and substance of Nairobi seem to survive intact. It may be physically Blacker now than when it started in 1969, but it is also more pragmatic, more self-confident, and less preoccupied with ideological or exclusively racial considerations. It may yet become stuck between the reef of academics and the rock of activism, but its professed intention is to give people the necessary skills for community reformation, and it has kept to that mission in spite of the temptations of various ideological world views (Black nationalism, pan-Africanism, third-world unity), and in spite of the pressures for conformity from the white majority.

Nairobi may not last forever, but it did not set out to become an institution for the ages; and as long as it can take care of business without succumbing to the human tendency to make self-preservation the first priority, it will probably continue to build an impressive record of service. Certainly not every college could do what Nairobi is doing. It may even be true that no established institution could survive such a radical alteration. But new institutions serving particular communities could learn much from the East Palo Alto experience. Nairobi is not only an alternative college; it is also an ad hoc institution, existing for a specific purpose until its task is finished. It is an idea worth repeating.

DQU

Peter A. Janssen

DQU is not a typical university, but then it is not trying to serve the typical university student. Its student body consists of about one hundred dropouts, migrants, kids from reservations and East Los Angeles, and anybody else who walks onto its campus, a former army communications base six miles west of Davis, California. It is the first university of its kind in the United States: half American Indian and half Chicano; and it is designed to be fully independent. It has no ties to other institutions—or to most current practices in American higher education. Students can stay for two years and get an Associate of Arts degree or for two weeks and get a certificate. They get credit for taking the usual array of college courses—and for participating in tribal dances or planting corn. In the past, the administration got food for the student cafeteria by trading grass grown on campus for meat slaughtered by a nearby farmer, and sheep still graze just outside the administration building.

The university, which registered its first class in September 1971, was a long time coming. It traces back to the early 1960s, when Jack D. Forbes, a Powhatan Indian with a Ph.D. in history and anthropology from the University of Southern California, started talking with Carl Gorman, the Navajo artist, about the need for an all-Indian institution. Forbes turned the conversations into position papers while he taught at Berkeley; in 1968 he persuaded the Donner Foundation to give him a small grant to study the feasibility of an Indian school.

During this period David Risling, Jr., a Hupa Indian who had been working at Modesto Junior College for twenty years, was elected president of the new California Indian Education Association. At one of its first meetings, the association asked Risling to try to find surplus government land for an Indian college. Most of the association's members were from rural communities and wanted Risling to look in rural areas in the central part of the state. According to Risling, who says that the Bureau of Indian Affairs once considered his father, an early advocate of Indian legal rights, "the most radical Indian in the United States," the idea for DQ started when people around the community became discouraged with the present educational system.

> *It didn't do anything to meet the needs of Indian people. It was very detrimental to the dignity of Indian people. Even if you made it through the system and stayed in school, you were insulted 90 percent of the time. You almost had to forget your culture because you were taught it was wrong.*
>
> *The big problem in school was that so many Indian kids were alienated. They didn't have the right dress; they didn't have enough money to buy the right styles or shoes. They had to fight with their parents for money and the parents had to decide whether to feed the family or buy clothes for school. The girls got pregnant and the boys fought. The teachers didn't understand them or their culture. Everything about school turned them off. Then in the sixties the civil rights thing came along big and people started to look at themselves. Indians got fed up and began to take things into their own hands.*

Realizing that at least some of the problem was in teachers' attitudes, the Indian Education Association started special workshops for teachers. Then minority groups banded together to promote a resolution, passed by the state legislature, that promoted courses in Black, Native American, and Chicano studies in state colleges.

In July 1969 Forbes, then thirty-five, came to the University of California at Davis to start a Native American studies program. Risling followed. They quickly teamed up with Chicano educators at Davis to start a library, and it was the beginning of a permanent alliance. The Indians and Chicanos discovered that the Davis administration was only too happy to leave them alone. "We found that the university was not interested in the program," Risling says. "They let us have just a little tokenism to keep us quiet. All of a sudden ecology was the big word; there was no money for the Native American studies program. Then a lot of other people—faculty—at Davis felt we were stepping on their toes. The anthropologists and historians were upset when we challenged their books or when kids brought in the real facts. The administration promised us a research unit and everything else. But they stalled and lost interest. We couldn't find out what happened. Then they put pressure on us and started to clamp down. We couldn't do the things we wanted to do. If we wanted to start a Native American music course, they said the music department should do it. Finally we decided we had to have control of our own institution."

Other Indians and Chicanos also were disenchanted with Davis. They thought that it served only the dominant Anglo culture and fostered an elitism that was hostile to their communities. They wanted to break away.

To be sure, the Indian-Chicano alliance was a marriage of convenience, since they were more powerful as a group than alone, but it also was a bonding of two groups whose cultures and aspirations were different from the atmosphere on the Davis campus. Leaders of each group believed that their cultures and history had far more in common with each other than with Anglo society. And neither had been able to start a college of its own.

They were in the right spot. In the summer of 1970 the Government Service Administration declared a 647-acre former army communications center, six miles west of Davis on Route 31, as government surplus. Most of the base was rich, flat farmland with a small cluster of ten buildings, constructed in 1953, and scores of telephone poles. It was up for public bid.

The Indian-Chicano forces regrouped as DQU and made a bid; so did half a dozen other organizations, including UC-Davis, which wanted the site for monkey experiments. DQ got some strong political allies, including John Tunney, then a congressman running successfully for the Senate. By November 3, 1970, the other organizations had dropped out; only Davis opposed DQ for the land.

That day a group of young Indians "occupied" the abandoned site. A month later, with the Indians still there and DQ threatening to fight Davis in court, Davis withdrew its bid. On April 2, 1971, the title was deeded over to DQ, and the new university had a campus. It was the first time that government surplus land had been granted to Indians or Chicanos for a school.

The campus still carries indications of its former life. Large signs say that some buildings are "off limits" to enlisted personnel. One parking space is still "reserved for executive officer," although a few feet away an old school bus is parked, with "Viva La Causa" painted on its side. Two large signs at the main gate have been repainted. At first they announced "Universidad Deganawidah Quetzalcoatl" in red and brown letters. Deganawidah was the founder of the Iroquois federation of nations, and Quetzalcoatl was the Aztec patron of the arts. The name was changed, however, when an Iroquois chief flew out from the East Coast to explain that the Iroquois considered it virtually sacrilegious to use the name of a deceased chief except during religious ceremonies or in a time of emergency. The signs and stationery were changed. The name of the institution became simply DQU.

Power at the school is divided equally among a thirty-two-member board of directors selected by leaders of Indian and Chicano community organizations in northern and central California. There are sixteen Native Americans on the board and sixteen Chicanos. Risling, head of Native American studies at Davis, is chairman; and Louis Flores, an engineer who is head of Chicano studies at Davis, is vice-chairman. Ultimately DQ's founders hope that the school will be governed by a board elected annually by Native Americans and Chicanos across the United States. In 1971 the board hired José de la Isla, an administrator with the American Association of Junior Colleges in Washington, to be DQ's executive director, or president. De la Isla returned to Washington after a year and was replaced by Leroy V. Clifford, a thirty-year-old Oglala Sioux who had been a consultant to many tribes on economic development.

Tuition at DQ is twenty dollars a unit; but finances, like almost everything else at the college, are informal. Students are urged to pay what they can; most come with grants from the Equal Opportunity Grants Program. Everyone is welcome at DQ; the only requirement is a desire to learn something. DQ opened as a two-year community college. It has correspondent status from the Western Association of Schools and Colleges and is recognized as a degree-granting (A.A.) institution by the state.

If all goes according to plan, by 1977 DQ will consist of four colleges with an enrollment of 1500. The first college, Tiburcio Vasquez, is already operating. It emphasizes the trades, agriculture, forestry, and small-business administration. The second, Hehaka Sapa (black elk), will deal with special Indian concerns such as water rights. The third, Quetzalcoatl, will concentrate on Chicano issues. The fourth, named after the doctor Carlos Montezuma, will train paramedics and nurses to carry health services to Indians and Chicanos.

In addition to its special emphasis, Tiburcio Vasquez offers the usual community college courses in mathematics, history, the humanities, and the natural and social sciences, but all the courses have a Native American or Chicano orientation. A natural science class, for example, studies tribal mind-altering techniques; a history class traces the flow of migrant farm labor. As might be suspected, DQ is not the place to come for formal lectures. The five full-time faculty members hold classes when they and their students want— for as long as they want. Throughout the college some courses are taught for credit and some are not. Many classes start and just keep going; people come in whenever they are ready. Grading is exclusively on a "pass" or "superior" basis; no one is stamped a failure.

The college also has developed a "contract" system of education, where the student stipulates what he or she wants to learn and how fast he or she wants to learn it. For the more advanced courses, the student signs a contract with a three-member contract committee, which consists of a DQ faculty member, a person who is an expert in the field under study, and another student who is working at the same level.

With the help of a $3,100,000 contract with the United States Department of Labor, DQ also is operating four community centers—at Blythe, Fresno, Stockton, and Modesto—for the basic education and retraining of migrant workers. By the start of 1973 the centers were holding classes for 550 farm workers in cooperative farming, bilingual skills, auto mechanics, household appliance repair, and nursing.

Jim Racine, director of DQ's North American studies, says that the school is aimed at students from reservations and migrant camps. "We want kids who never thought of going to college," he says, "who probably wouldn't get in anyplace else. We're looking for people who will return home and use their education for the benefit of their community, assist those behind them."

In the spirit of building a new community, everyone works at DQ. Students sit on all committees; they also perform much of the menial labor associated with keeping an institution going. They help with the sheep, the bakery, and the kiln that can make adobe for other buildings as they are needed.

To date, DQ's greatest problem is its small financial base. The university has received $200,000 from the Office of Economic Opportunity plus $70,000 from the Office of Education to get it started, and its founders hope that Indian colleges will get some kind of congressional appropriation. They consider DQ a land-grant institution and feel that Black colleges are receiving a great deal of emphasis, money, and media attention while Indians and Chicanos are comparatively ignored.

Forbes readily describes the difficulties he and Risling have faced: "The problem with starting something new," he says, "is that it doesn't fit into the bureaucracy of higher education. Most legislation, most accrediting agencies, most educational systems are not geared to learning; they're geared to a structure and a sequence of events. You attend a certain number of classes, a certain number of events, and you get a number of grades. In trying to get DQ started and qualified for aid, we were up against that procedure. It's so foreign to what we're trying to do. It makes it very difficult for a new school to be innovative."

DQ wants new kinds of college students, and Forbes realistically expects them to bring some problems. He describes three groups of Indian and Chicano students:

> *One type is Chicano from East Los Angeles or Indian from urban areas or from disorganized reservations. They tend to have negative attitudes to education. The fact that they come to DQ means something, but their basic attitudes are negative. Many have severe social and psychological problems—drugs, drinking, fighting, hostility. Back at home they might be classified as hoods; they're pretty rough, maybe they have a record. They're the type of population that a white school is not confronted with because it doesn't want to serve the socially marginal individual. DQ wants to try to meet the needs of this group. But it has to use unique approaches to do it.*
>
> *The second group is the more traditional Indian student, regardless of age, who's still an Indian. He's the real thing. These students tend to be easy to work with. They're polite, with the traditional Indian virtues of sincerity, honesty, and so forth. They present a problem only in that they'd probably flunk out of a white school.*
>
> *The third group is the normal, middle-class, stable group of Indians and Chicanos who make it through white schools. This is a small group. The problem they present for DQ is that they are very anxious now to become more Indian and Chicano, to recover their heritage and sense of being. They want to be more like the second group.*
>
> *Now when you mix the third group with the first group, you've got trouble. The first group cannot attack the second group because the second group represents the real people—they know the Indian songs, the values, the roles. But the first group can attack the third group, because the third group represents white values. White colleges avoid the conflict because they restrict their admissions to group number three. But DQ has to develop an educational program suitable for these diverse groups.*

Forbes says that when the groups have been thrown together, such as during the occupation of Alcatraz or demonstrations in Los Angeles, the first group was so hostile that it eventually drove away the other two.

Forbes's philosophy will influence what happens at DQ. "The important thing about education," he says, "is that an individual has to develop himself and make key decisions himself. There's no way in the world you can force a person to be a good person. A white college thinks it can force a person to be a well-rounded, civilized person. One could easily prove they have not been successful in this. At DQ we try a different system, where an individual works out his own programs and where he can stay with something, if he wants to, until he masters it. The important thing is individual accomplishment, not the time spent. If one student can do something in two years, that's fine. If it takes somebody else four years, that's fine too. When he's ready, we'll test his mastery of the subject—perhaps by an oral exam, a written exam, or something else."

Mike Ginnett is typical of DQ's freewheeling approach to higher education. A former mountain pack guide who spent six years in California prisons after a burglary conviction, Ginnett now takes some courses in Native American literature, helps out in the small day-care center for the children of students and faculty, and also helps plan Hehaka Sapa College. "DQ is about the best thing that's happened to me," Ginnett says.

Another student, Kathy Koskela, came to DQ as part of an independent-study project during her junior year at the University of California at Santa Cruz. She was majoring in Native American literature, "and all of a sudden I found that nobody at Santa Cruz knew anything more about it than I did. So I came here." Kathy, a member of the Wylaki tribe in Northern California, also does some teaching at DQ while completing her own work.

The key to DQ is its emphasis on meeting each student where he is—and then helping him get where he wants to go. "DQ is a place where Chicanos and Indians can come and blossom like flowers," says Executive Director Clifford. "The students are finding their own cultural identity. From now on, DQ will be a place where

people can come and learn the things they really want to learn—
not the things the dominant white system imposes on them."

🐚 Navajo Community College 🐚

Peter A. Janssen

Until 1969, when Navajo Community College started classes
in some extra rooms borrowed from a Bureau of Indian Affairs
high school in Many Farms, Arizona, most young Indians had nowhere to go for a higher education. To understand the need for the
college, one must understand the depths of poverty, poor education,
and isolation on the Navajo reservation. The average family income
on the reservation itself (home for about 125,000 Navajos) is
$1500 a year. Fully one third of the adults do not read or speak
English. The average adult (over 25) has spent less than five years
in formal school. And the reservation is a nation unto itself, stretch-
ing across the northeastern corner of Arizona and into parts of New
Mexico and Utah. The college is about a half mile north of Many
Farms, a cluster of small homes, trailers, and a gas station in the
midst of a high plateau. Brown, orange, and red mesas rise to the
west; buzzards float through a pale blue sky overhead. Many Farms
is about ten miles north of Chinle (a larger town, with a variety
store and a motel); seventy-two miles from Window Rock, the seat
of the Navajo tribal government; and twenty-five miles from
Gallup, the closest real town (population 14,089), just across the
state line—and off the reservation—in New Mexico.

The reservation may be remote from the outside world, but
the outside world still exerts its control on the minds—and money—
of the Navajos. The Navajo tribal council—the governing body
elected by the tribe—operates as a demigovernment on the reservation, supervising its own police force and starting its own economic-
development programs. But the elementary and secondary schools
are run by the BIA, and most teachers and principals are Anglos.
Most official and professional jobs on the reservation are held by
Anglos. There is only one Navajo medical doctor on the reservation
and only two Navajo lawyers.

In 1968 the tribal council, influenced partly by the demands of Blacks to run their own institutions and partly by a desperate desire to improve educational levels on the reservation, decided to start a Navajo-run, Navajo-controlled two-year college. The council had at least one precedent. A few years earlier the Navajos had persuaded the BIA to let them set policies at Rough Rock Demonstration Elementary School about twenty miles west of Many Farms. That experiment seemed to be working well.

The council hired Ned A. Hatathli, a forty-eight-year-old Navajo and chairman of the board of Rough Rock School, as the college president; and Robert A. Rossel, Jr., an Anglo administrator who had set up Rough Rock, as college chancellor. Hatathli got money from OEO, the tribe, the Donner Foundation, and some private donors and opened the college for 301 students in January 1969.

Navajo Community College is not a particularly innovative school; indeed, it is almost traditional in the way it approaches teaching and learning. But it is important because of where it is— in the midst of the largest Indian reservation in the United States— and because it is under local control. It also is significant because of the size of the vacuum it is trying to fill. "The unique thing about this school," Hatathli says, "is that Indian people have control." He hopes that the college "will be a stepping stone for Indian young people from high school to a four-year institution. You know, 90 percent of our people don't go anywhere after high school. A lot of them just don't know what to do. They'll have a better chance of competing after two years here. They'll have a better chance at completing four years of college somewhere else, or of learning meaningful skills, competing for jobs."

Ultimately, the college is responsible to the elected tribal council. But college policies are set by the college's board of regents, appointed by the council. All ten regents are Navajo men; one is seventy years old, has never been to school in his life, and speaks no English. Hatathli, in turn, is responsible to the regents.

Hatathli is almost typecast for the job. Born in a hogan on Coal Mine Mesa on the reservation, he started as a sheepherder, spent two years taking commercial courses at Haskell Institute in Lawrence, Kansas, and finally got a B.S. degree from Arizona State College. He then became manager of the Navajo Arts and Crafts

Guild (the showcase for the tribe's handicrafts) in Window Rock, was elected to the tribal council in 1955, and ultimately became its director of resources.

So far, things have gone well for the college. In the fall of 1971 tribal officials broke ground for the college's permanent campus—a 12,000-acre gift from the tribe on Tsaile Lake, thirty miles east of Many Farms. The new campus (costing about $14,000,000, with the largest chunks of money from HUD, the BIA, and the tribe itself) is scheduled to open in 1974. Until then, the college makes do in borrowed rooms in the two-story, factory-like, pea-green BIA high school in Many Farms. Hatathli's office is across the parking lot from the school, in a trailer. The college's student union (with a small short-order counter, a few booths, and two pool tables) is in an adjacent trailer.

President Hatathli hopes that Congress will appropriate funds, on a formula basis, to support the college. He and many other Indians in higher education frequently point out that Howard University receives a large amount of operating money each year from Congress because of its special arrangement with the federal government; they think there should be at least one Indian institution with a similar appropriation. This year the college's operating budget is about $1,300,000. The largest portions are $730,000 from OEO, $250,000 from the tribe, and $100,000 from the Donner Foundation.

Students must pay about $555 each semester if they live in dorms (and 196 of the 300 full-time students do). That includes $200 for tuition, $120 for room, $150 for a five-day meal ticket (or $200 for a seven-day ticket), and more for books and incidentals. About 80 percent of the students now enrolled at NCC receive some type of aid through various state, federal, and BIA programs.

The college does not have any entrance requirements, except that a student must be at least eighteen years old if he is not a high school graduate. (In fact, 85 percent of the students now are high school graduates.) It offers four basic programs: (1) college-level courses leading to the A.A. degree or to transfer to a four-year institution; (2) vocational-technical courses, such as auto mechanics, welding, nursing, drafting, and home economics; (3) Navajo studies, ranging from Navajo history and culture to Navajo silver-smithing (all Navajo students must take at least nine credits); (4) a precollege program with heavy emphasis on English and mathematics. In addition, the college offers adult courses (taught by five Navajos) in fifteen spots across the reservation. The grading system is H (honors), P (pass), D (deferred or incomplete), N (no credit, or, as the catalog states, "not a failing grade"), and A (audit). The college has correspondent status with the North Central Association of Colleges and Secondary Schools, the usual probationary status for new schools.

About one third of the thirty-four full-time faculty members are Navajos. Hatathli says that the others keep their jobs "with the understanding that they are to work themselves out of a job. I would like to see more Navajo people on the faculty, but at the same time I want to see the quality of instruction remain high." The college has not yet had to recruit faculty. "Word got out the first year that we were an Indian institution," Hatathli says. "It was sort of romantic. Everybody wants to see what they can do to help an Indian institution. We got lots of do-gooders, you know." Most instructors live in Many Farms, in trailers or houses rented from the BIA.

The students are traditional early 1950s: boys with short hair and neat clothes, usually jeans and sport shirts; girls in modest dresses. The only antiwar activity dates to Custer, not Cambodia. And formidable-appearing signs in the dorms warn that male and female students are definitely to be separate, with a total curfew at 11 P.M., Sunday through Thursday, and 2 A.M. on Friday and Saturday. Students' rooms are inspected each week. The only signs of a counterculture (or of a modern college campus) were a few trying-to-be-hip members of the faculty.

Many day-to-day decisions at the college are made by the college council, an all-Navajo organization composed of four members of the faculty, four members of the administration, and four students. Council members, elected by their own groups on campus, make policy recommendations to Hatathli, who says that he respects them. The college also has the normal array of committees: a selection committee, a curriculum committee, an academic committee, a library committee, and an accreditation committee. The personnel committee interviews all candidates for jobs and makes recommendations to Hatathli. He has never gone against their recommendations.

The greatest problem with the college at first, according to Hatathli, was "a general lack of planning. The OEO made money available at the end of 1968 and told us we had to open doors right away. We started in January 1969, in mid-year, and had a lot of settling-down problems. Most of the students who came in January were between jobs or just hanging around. The same was true with the faculty. There was a high turnover; we lost forty to sixty students. In the 1970–71 school year, our first full year, the students were more serious. Only about 15 percent dropped out. We did lots of planning then, but we're still not really settled as far as the curriculum is concerned."

Hatathli and other administrators at NCC emphasize that Navajo students need lots of tutoring and counseling to help them adjust to college life. "The problem with students," Hatathli says, "is that in their home environment practically no English is spoken. There is no conversation in English, just Navajo. They have no opportunity to study, no electric lights. Most children in high school outside an Indian reservation have electric lights; they don't have to work for their next meal. These are conveniences we don't have on the Indian reservation. So our students have problems, and they need counseling and tutoring."

Across the parking lot, one wing of the high school serves as the college's temporary administration building. Jack C. Jackson, dean of student personnel services, like Hatathli, was born on the reservation. He came to NCC from the public school in Window Rock (the difference between a public school and a BIA school on the reservation is that a BIA school has dorms), where he was head basketball coach. He signed on thinking he would be basketball coach at the college, but it does not yet have a team, and Jackson just teaches physical education.

"We don't expect to go out and recruit top-notch students here," he says. "A kid like that can go to the University of New Mexico or Arizona State, and that's fine if the student is capable of pulling it off. So we're getting students whose second or third choice of college is Navajo Community College. When we opened, we had some problems with students' attitude because of this. And we had to postpone basketball—you can't ask top-notch athletes to come here when we don't have facilities." The college shares the BIA high school gym at what seems to be the high school's convenience.

Jackson says that NCC must set up a curriculum that ties together both the Navajo culture and the culture of the rest of society.

> *We want to control our own affairs and at the same time take advantage of the useful things in the dominant society. We can't go back and live like our ancestors did fifty or a hundred years ago. We're not prepared to live that type of life. We're used to electricity and the automobile now. The curriculum committee is working on a curriculum that will be acceptable to the Navajo people, but trying to involve parents is difficult. They have never had an opportunity to be involved in education before, and now they don't know what to do. The students too, coming from BIA schools, have had little opportunity to make an impact on the operation of their school, and some of them have trouble adjusting here. But we would like to see a student, when he leaves here, be familiar with Navajo culture, where there are some good teachings left, and combine them with some good teachings from Anglo society.*

Like many other Indians, Jackson believes that poor preparation in BIA schools is the cause of many students' problems.

> *The lack of preparation in reading and English is the main thing. And the curriculum has not been relevant to the Navajo people. The kid is taught English in school, but his parents don't speak English at home. There's a cultural gap and a generation gap. There are no courses in Indian studies in high school, so when kids go home their parents seem remote. The kids don't know what is going on. They don't even know what the dances are—they make fun*

*of their culture. They make fun of things that are supposed
to be sacred religious ceremonies.*

*So when we started NCC, many of the kids came
and said they wanted to know what was going on. They
asked about the dances. We tell them where they came
from. If we can tell the kids who they are, they will have a
better chance of making useful lives. We find that most
want to come here, get an education, go home to the reservation, get a job, and live with the people. That's good.
One purpose of Navajo Community College is to get people
to hold good jobs, to live both among the Navajo population and the dominant society. We hope they can get a
good enough education so they can do what they want.*

Across the hall from Jackson's office, Mordecai Abromowitz,
dean of instruction (needless to say, Abromowitz is not a Navajo),
is trying to put together a solid curriculum for NCC. The problem
is that under the founding concept of the college the curriculum
must be shaped by Navajos themselves. "The crucial innovation
here," Abromowitz says, "is that this school is run by Navajos.
The curriculum committee (all its members are Navajos) is trying
to bring in more Navajo members of the faculty and staff, to bring
in medicine men and other people from the community and ask
them what they think college is all about. We want the medicine
men, the elders, to say what they think the concerns of the college
should be. Navajo control means decisions made by Navajos."
Those decisions have not been made yet, even though the college
has been open since 1969. The curriculum is still standard community college fare, with a cultural twist. The school seems to want
fairly standard teachers, too. When a reporter asked Abromowitz
whether medicine men or elders might be brought in to teach a
course (as at DQU), he replied, "I don't think anyone like that
will be brought in with the thought of making him a teacher."

Most classes for the college are taught in a second-floor wing
of the high school. Most are small and relatively informal. In a
college-level English course recently, students were gathered around
a middle-aged Anglo female teacher for a vocabulary lesson. She

was reading a story set in the Middle East to illustrate the word *obliterate*. "If the wind blows and it obliterates the tracks of the Arabs, what does it mean?" she asked. After a moment a few students reponded that it meant "wiped out." In another part of the large classroom an older Anglo teacher was giving three students a basic arithmetic lesson in placing decimals. She was dividing 24 into 560 on the blackboard, and some of the kids were having trouble with it.

Down the hall Phil Reno was teaching a course in Navajo and Hopi resources to four students. He was on water rights ("The problem is that more people want water than there is water to go around"), and since this is a major political issue in the Southwest, the students were extremely interested. "The basic water rights," Reno said, "are Indian rights. But the water has to be for beneficial use, and the way the courts have determined that is if it makes money, it is beneficial. That may not be a good way to look at it, but that's the way it is." The kids nodded agreement.

In the room next door, Richard Begay, NCC's twenty-six-year-old student-body president, sat alone, doing some homework. Begay went to the BIA school in Sherman, spent three years in the army, and then worked for a heavy-equipment operator off the reservation. "When I got out of the army, I had the intention of going back to school," he said. "I looked around but I could not compete at other universities. I had financial problems too, so I tried this." Begay entered NCC in January 1971 and manages to stay afloat with money from the G.I. Bill. He wants to get an A.A. in accounting and go on to Arizona State. He thinks he's lucky to be in school. "I wonder how many people like me can't go back to school and just turn into drunks in Gallup because they can't compete," he said. "Lots of my friends dropped out. They think they don't have the ability to do it. For them—now they just get drunk." Many Navajos, Begay says, simply get turned off by the BIA schools. He is still angry that he had to learn Spanish as a foreign language in high school: "I told them that for me English was a foreign language. Navajo was my real language."

Like many other students, Begay plans to stay on the reservation when he gets out of school. "It depends on where I'm being needed," he says. "I'd rather help my people help themselves. We've got to work to help ourselves at home first before we tackle big things."

Begay lives in an apartment in Many Farms with a friend, but most NCC students live in the college dorm, next to the three high school dorms, at the north end of the campus. Two adult counselors—both Navajos—have offices there, one for males, one for females. Margaret Etsitty, one of the counselors, says that the entering students have numerous personal problems, "usually having to do with their family":

> *They are caught between two societies. Many really don't know how to go to school. They graduate from high school and they don't know what to do. What if they fail? They really aren't ready to go to college. Lots of their families think they should go to work, stay home and help with the farms.*
>
> *They have a great problem of self-identity; they're not sure where they belong, and other problems, like drinking, follow after that. Drinking is all around here. It's illegal on the reservation, but ask anybody, go to any activity, and you'll see a lot of it going on. A lot of young people are heading toward becoming alcoholics.*
>
> *Trying to help them—almost all of them—is a problem. It's pretty hard for them to come in and talk with the counselors. Lots of our students don't know too much about counseling. In boarding school they only saw the counselor when they were in trouble. So we have some students who act as counselor aides to go between us and the students. We try to put the emphasis on helping students here so they won't feel threatened by anything.*

It is still too early to tell how much Navajo Community College is helping students. Clearly, it is offering several hundred young people an opportunity at postsecondary education that did not exist before. And the school probably will become stronger, with a clearer picture of purpose and curriculum, once it moves out of the shadow of the BIA high school and onto its own campus.

The college's facilities now are meager. The library, for

example, has only 15,000 volumes and squeezes by in the far end of the high school library. Student areas are almost barren of books and magazines; the campus is empty of much of the music and noise and activities that make most colleges such special places for the young. But then Navajo Community College is a very special place. "This is the first college open to Navajos," says student-body president Begay, "and it's difficult for all of us. The college today is only a baby. It's got a lot of growing up to do."

Pima College
John Egerton

The tipoff on Pima College is its first catalog, an eighty-page booklet with an odd shape (eight and a half inches square), an array of artistic symbols, and twenty-one full-page photographs worthy of inclusion in Edward Steichen's *Family of Man*. Parts of the catalog are printed in both English and Spanish. Admission, it says, is available to any person upon completion of an official application form—no minimum age, no high school graduation requirement, no standardized tests. The cost to residents of Tucson and surrounding Pima County is sixty dollars a semester, and financial aid is available. There are over four hundred courses to choose from, beginning with air conditioning, art, auto mechanics, and behavioral sciences and running through speech, Swahili, tool and machine technology, and welding.

On page 6 the catalog states, "Pima College is committed to the concept of a pluralistic society." There follows a description of the college's intercultural committee, made up of "representatives of the four major groups in Pima County—Indians, Mexican-Americans, Anglos, and Blacks—and of the varying points of view within each of those groups." And on page 2, in a statement of philosophy, these sentences appear: "Each individual in the Pima College community is encouraged to take pride in his own heritage and at the same time to develop awareness and appreciation of differences which stem from differing backgrounds. An institution committed to these ends attempts to create an atmosphere rich in a diversity of subject matter, materials, and educational approaches.

In accepting the principle of continuous and open evaluation of all activities, the college will encourage all participants to make free, intelligent, and responsible choices from a wide range of alternatives."

Pima is trying to give substance not only to the concept of cultural pluralism but also to some other hallowed—and often hollow—ideals: it is trying to be an institution whose first responsibility is to its students, it is trying to serve the community, and it is trying to practice participatory democracy. Any college that is really serious about such matters is on a precarious mission—some would say dangerous, or even misguided. It is one thing to *talk* about them, but to build them into the structure, to make them central to the college's success or failure, is something else. There is no assurance that it will work, but there are many administrators and faculty members at Pima whose primary reason for coming there was to give those principles a try.

Pima is a two-year community college on the western edge of Tucson. Opened to students in the fall of 1970, it gets virtually all of its more than $7,700,000 in annual operating and capital revenues from the county (70 percent) and the state. Because Pima is a congeries of humanity, the potential for conflict is everywhere: between the college and the city; between whites and Blacks and browns and red and yellows, and within those groups; between militant and moderate, hip and straight; between liberal-arts and vocational-technical advocates; between the college and the University of Arizona, a multiversity on the other side of the city; between faculty innovators and traditionalists; between the college and the parents, with their first-generation students caught in beween. With all that diversity, though, there has been relatively little actual conflict.

Table 1 shows an estimate of the racial makeup of the college and the community in 1971.

Those figures are based on estimates and approximations— in such a place it is not always easy to tell a person's race just by looking—but they are at least reasonably accurate. (A questionnaire distributed at registration asks students to indicate the racial group "with which you most closely identify yourself." There are 33 choices, ranging from African, Afro-American, Black, Brown,

Table 1. Racial Composition of Pima County and
Pima College, 1971

	Anglo	Chicano	Black	Indian	Oriental
Pima County population	70%	20%	6%	3%	1%
Pima College Enrollment	67	23	7	2	1
Administration	79	9	9	0	3
Faculty	73	16	7	2	2
Nonacademic staff	46	36	10	7	1

and Chicano through Papago, Pima, Spanish, White, and Yaqui, and all the possible combinations of the basic groups. There was no choice on the list that was passed over by all of the students, but more than 200 of them opted for number 34: "Other.") Such a combination of people didn't just happen—it was made to happen, not by the imposition of quotas but by the determination of the board of governors and the administration to have what Kenneth Harper (who was president of the college until 1972) calls "a critical mass." That has meant intensive recruiting, an occasional "freeze" on white faculty, and in some cases a salary bonus for sought-after minorities. These practices have often infuriated many Tucson Anglos, and some whites have threatened to sue the college on the grounds that they are being discriminated against because of their race. On more than one occasion Harper has taken to television to defend his policies, and people began to realize that pluralism at Pima is more than just a word. Still, there are limits: Harper put off filling three administrative positions for several months, hoping to get minority applicants for the jobs, but his board finally directed him not to wait any longer, and all three of the jobs went to whites.

The board of governors itself is made up of four white men and one Mexican-American woman, all elected; and there are four nonvoting members—two faculty members and two students. Until late in 1971 the board met weekly—once a month to take official actions, the other times for study sessions. Michael J. Brown, the board's president, is a thirty-seven-year-old lawyer who believes firmly in what Pima is trying to do, and in fact is one of the principal architects of its policies. "We've got everything but Polish dock workers here," he says with a smile, "and my Polish wife says she's going to do something about that." Brown, "a WASP who graduated from Notre Dame," is a former policeman who has lived in Tucson for fifteen years. He likes Pima's openness: "This is the place for society to make its investment. We take anybody—the dropouts, the ex-cons, you name it. Otherwise, you pay later—in law enforcement, in the courts and the jails, in welfare."

Pima is not the only college in the country that will "take anybody," but few schools buttress their open-admissions policy with as much encouragement and support. The students range in age from sixteen to seventy-two; their average age is about twenty-five. All but a handful come from Pima County, and nearly half of them receive some type of financial aid. Many of the students have not finished high school, and a few have not gone beyond elementary school; but Harper believes that 95 percent of those who enroll can move successfully through a two-year program. It will be awhile before student retention can be measured, but the first indication is encouraging: 80 percent of all those enrolled in the first semester were back for the second semester. Enrollment reached almost 6000 in the fall of 1971—a 50 percent increase over the first fall semester.

There is no doubt that Pima is an attractive place to the students. They are represented on every committee in the college, they have a veritable supermarket of a curriculum to choose from, they have a no-fail grading system, they have an opportunity to rate the faculty, they are not subjected to an overabundance of rules and regulations and punishments. Campus security officers dress in uniforms that do not look like uniforms, carry two-way radios but no weapons, are trained to assist students instead of harassing them—and the chief security officer was chosen by the students themselves. "We have not had a problem with drugs on this campus," a member of the board of governors says, "and one of the main reasons for that is the nonrepressive style of the security staff. They have given the students a lot of responsibility for self-policing, and the students have responded with self-restraint. They know a bust would bring a clampdown from the city police, and they don't want anybody messing over their college, so they've kept the place pretty clean."

There have been no racial incidents, either. In the hallways and courtyards of the college, the diversity of the student body is evident everywhere, and casual clusters of students seem more often than not to be multiracial. According to the director of student activities, Diego Navarrette, the cross-cultural activity is spontaneous. "We've had no severe confrontations of any kind involving race," he says. "There may even be too little conflict—but it's nice. There is so much variety in ethnic groups, and the different cultures and life-styles are so much a part of this place, that there has been no need for separatism. It could all fall apart tomorrow, but right now the kids seem to groove on it."

Navarrette is a good example of the kind of person Pima has sought—and often found—for its faculty and staff. A native of Tucson and a great-grandson of a soldier of fortune who rode with Pancho Villa, he has been around a good bit himself. As a youngster he was processed through a government-sponsored program of "Americanization" designed to replace his native language and culture. He did graduate work in linguistics at UCLA. He has taught in a rural school for Mormons and in his own high school, Pueblo, in Tucson. And for a time he was an ardent nationalist in the brown power–Chicano power movement. Of that he says simply, "I've had a value change. It was pulling me apart, and I was getting nothing from it. I sympathize with the movement—it is still the only way for some—but for me, the nationalistic line is too short-range. It is building boundaries, and boundaries won't work. I don't have time—this world doesn't have time—to deal in a nationalistic bag. Pluralism could be just another dead end, but the ideas behind it are not. I think that's our only chance in the society of the future, and as long as Pima is moving in that direction I'll stick around."

A similarly expressed commitment to pluralism is heard time and again in conversations with faculty and staff. John Barnes, a white professor of humanities, talks about it when he describes his year on the intercultural committee. Grover Banks, a Black man from Ohio who heads the federally funded Student Special Services program, calls what Pima is trying "the last ditch. We're trying to retain all of the old cultures and also create a new one. Whether you focus first on similarities and then move to an appreciation of differences or whether you go the other way around, it's a risky business." Henry Oyama, director of the college's bilingual institute, speaks with pride of his own multicultural heritage—his father was Japanese and his mother Chicano—and calls the Pima experiment "far from perfect, but the best I've found." Mike Enis, a Papago Indian, gave up a secure civil service job to become a welding instructor at Pima "because I owe it to our young people. I can give them a role model, show them that it is possible to have the best of both worlds—this one, and the one that centers around the tribe. Some of the elders in my tribe think I am a deserter, a cop-out, but I believe pluralism is the only way. It's why I came here. It *has* to work." And Herman Warrior, a Black who heads the student-development faculty (counseling and other supportive services), admits the difficulties of working with so many different kinds of students but says confidently, "It's going to work. The commitment is here—all we need is time and tolerance. I'm here to see if we can make it; if we can't, it's all down the tube."

One of the best things Pima has going for it is the curriculum. In both its organization and its content, it seems varied, flexible, and imaginative. The vocational and technical subject matter is not treated as a separate part of the college but is inter-related with the liberal arts and sciences. Drafting, electronics, and computer science, for example, are tied through several courses to mathematics, physics, and engineering. The same is true of general business, management, and office education. Respiratory therapy, X-ray technology, nursing, and health care are considered extensions of some parts of chemistry and the life sciences. Pima also trains technicians for the electronic and print media; tradesmen in welding, tool and machine technology, sheet metal, air conditioning, and auto mechanics; and specialists in law enforcement, home economics, and fire science. In all of these, both faculty members and students are full and equal partners in the Pima community.

For each of the four major racial groups at Pima there are courses that stress cultural identity. For whites there are the standard English literature and Western civilization. For Indians there are courses in behavioral sciences and history that are of particular interest, and there are also courses in the Papago language. Blacks can take Swahili, African art, African and Afro-American history, and Afro-American literature. Chicanos, the largest minority group, can find a number of courses taught in Spanish as well as Mexican-American art, history, drama, dance, and literature.

Cross-cultural and pluralistic understanding and involvement are emphasized in more than a score of courses, including art, music, anthropology, history, and politics. There is a course in ethnic theater, one in economic development for minority groups, one in human development and interpersonal relationships, another in ethics and social philosophy, one on human relations in business and industry, and others on such subjects as community organization and development, ghetto society, explorations in prejudice, civil rights practices, and United States social problems. Police-community relations, cultural history of sports, oral communication among various cultures, comparative religions, and immigration laws and practices also are taught.

Beyond all these, there are courses with such titles as Sociology of Utopia ("the study of alternative life-styles"), Plain Writing ("practical experience in solving individual everyday writing problems"), Potpourri ("from auto mechanics to Zen meditation"), Learning Team ("a chance to explore ideas and experiences in many different areas of study, work, cultural awareness, and community involvement"), and Political Revolution and Violence ("how violent changes in political power come about"). There are also some basic and very imaginative courses in reading and writing, and in physics there is even a course called How Things Work (your iron, your thermometer, your telephone).

By deemphasizing required courses and encouraging exploration and freedom of choice, Pima provides students access to virtually any subject through a variety of approaches. Some courses are programmed for individualized self-study, and credit can be earned by examination. The Exploratory Program and Student Learning Teams are two kinds of organized activities built around a sampling of courses, ideas, and experiences and small-group cooperative ventures.

Perhaps the most creative aspect of the instructional program is something called the learning-unit system, a method developed by

James Lowell, a Pima botanist, and other faculty members. It is a means of breaking down the separation between subject areas and between courses within a given area. To understand how it works, here is an example from the social sciences:

In this interdisciplinary area (there are no separate departments), each subject—sociology, psychology, political science, history, anthropology—is put together in a package of related courses and broken down into units that focus on a particular topic. History, for example, includes its courses in United States, Papago, Mexican-American, and Afro-American history in one grouping, and then divides them into twenty-three core units (such as the American Revolution, the Frontier, the Era of Franklin D. Roosevelt) and thirty-six alternate units (including Mexican-American Immigration, Hiroshima, and the Embargo of 1807). Since each of the major subjects in the social sciences has a similar combination of units, the student thus has a choice of almost two hundred mini-courses. If he wants to concentrate on Papago history, he can earn three semester hours of credit by taking just that course; if he wants to range over the entire field of social studies, he can select six or seven or eight units, or as many as he feels he can handle, and get three hours of credit in the social sciences through the Exploratory Program. If he wants credit in history alone, he can select at least four core units and two or more alternate units from the history package and accomplish his objective. He builds his own schedule, and then signs up for the units he has selected. Successful completion of six units earns him a C grade for the semester, completion of seven results in a B, and eight earns an A.

Scheduling, obviously, is a very complicated process, and record keeping (computerized) is described by one faculty member as "horrendous." But the latitude afforded students is enormous, and the learning-unit system is very popular with them. It is constantly being modified and refined by the faculty; and, for all the confusion that sometimes accompanies that process, it is likely to remain a central part of the Pima curriculum.

Further impetus for a thoroughgoing integration of Pima's various components is found in the internal organization of the college. There is the college council, a twelve-member body (three each from the administration, faculty, student body, and nonacademic staff), which meets weekly with the president. There is the intercultural committee, now being reorganized into a human relations council with thirty-four members—elected by their colleagues from each of the college's "decision centers"—and a single director, instead of four, as the intercultural committee had. And then there is the physical structure of the college itself. On the outside Pima's new buildings seem stark and uninviting, huge masses of concrete in a sort of early-fortress architectural style. Inside they seem just the opposite. At President Harper's insistence, there are very few interior walls—no faculty carrels or offices behind opaque glass doors, no administrative sanctuaries or executive suites. Harper's own office is behind a shoulder-high partition in a corner of an enormous "administrative room," and none of the offices have locks, or even doors. The faculty, too, are dispersed in interdisciplinary clusters.

Time after time in Pima's short history, innovations have met strong resistance—from faculty or administrators, from the community, from one racial group or another. More often than not, that resistance has been generated by particular groups who wanted either to maintain an advantage or to seize one. Thus, the learning-unit system, student power, equality between the liberal and vocational instruction realms, priority hiring of minorities, one-man-one-vote parity for nonacademic employees, and of course pluralism have often angered and alienated somebody. But a consensus in the college family has been maintained so far, not only for the general direction in which it is moving but for most of the particulars as well. Whenever any of the more controversial decisions has come up for discussion, someone usually has said, "But we're just not ready for that." Harper has a stock response: "The way you get ready is to try."

If Pima has succeeded in selling the concept of pluralism to its white, brown, and Black constituents, it has been far less successful with Indians. There are about 10,000 Indians living in Pima County—Papagos, mostly, but also some from the Yaqui and Pima tribes, and a scattered few others; and as a group they are the most voiceless and destitute of the county's citizens. "Their way of life is totally alien to our understanding," says one administrator of the college. Another adds, "We simply don't know how to put the

Indian in an urban setting without being destructive of his culture."
Harper speaks of the need to "bring in enough of their culture to
make them feel at home," but the search for Indian faculty members and administrators—not to mention students—has been frus-
tratingly difficult and only minimally successful.

The Papagos live, for the most part, on reservations—perhaps 2000 on the edge of Tucson, and a much larger number on a
sprawling rural reservation about seventy-five miles to the west.
(Pima County covers more than 9000 square miles of mountain and
desert, and Tucson is its only city of any size.) Wherever the Indians
live, they are caught in the same trap: they are surrounded and
immobilized by an inhospitable society. However much Pima College may try to respect and preserve Indian culture, the college is
still part of another world—a dynamic, urbanized, technological
world. And any Indian who comes there and tries to be a cross-
cultural man is bound to feel intense conflict within himself. Mike
Enis, one of the three Papagos on the faculty, expresses the dilemma: "If it were not for this college, many of my people would
drift away from the reservations to distant cities—many of them do
anyway—and their ties with the tribe are broken, and they become
anonymous people, lost and broken. Yet to become educated,
skilled, is also a break with the tribal customs and traditions, and
many of the elders are opposed to it. It is a poor choice either way,
and so many of our young simply stay where they are, on the
reservation. They drop out—just like some young whites are doing."
Meanwhile, Pima continues to search for ways to make itself a more
attractive and satisfactory choice for the Indians it is pledged to
serve.

Tucson seems an unlikely place for the development of a
college like Pima. In spite of the presence of four large racial groups,
as well as the representation of Orientals, it is dominated by whites,
and it is, on the whole, a rather conservative community, if its
politics and its press can be taken as any sort of measuring rod.
Copper and aeronautics are the dominant industries, and a large air
force base and the University of Arizona are its dominant institutions. Segregation is evident in housing and schools, and among the
minorities there are relatively few professional people. For the most
part, the wealth is white wealth and the poverty is nonwhite poverty.

With all this, Pima has come to be seen as a mixed blessing in many quarters; and as its notions of pluralism and permissiveness and participatory democracy have spread, so have the misgivings and reservations of the city's ruling elite.

The University of Arizona did not oppose the development of a new public college at its doorstep. The university has grown rapidly in recent years and, with its emphasis on graduate instruction, has not been able to accommodate all of the prospective freshmen with good high school records and high test scores, let alone those whose credentials are deficient. Since Pima would be providing a chance in college for students the university would not take anyway, it seemed a good idea. But Pima is not only attracting students whom the university does not want; it is also becoming a popular choice for many who could enroll in the big institution but do not want to. In 1971 Pima had more freshmen from Pima County than the university did. If that trend continues—and if Pima is able to retain and educate a significant number of students who would have been rejected by the university as poor risks for success in college— the implications could be embarrassing for the university.

So the potential for friction between the university and its upstart neighbor across town is something to be reckoned with. That possibility, unfortunately, is not the only one in Tucson that could cause trouble for Pima. There is also the press, for example. Tucson's two daily newspapers have not been especially friendly to the college; in fact, in the view of a good many in the college community, they have been downright hostile. "They send reporters out here trying to find disenchanted students," one administrator says "and when they can't find any, they say we've brainwashed them."

A faculty member, noting the various and conflicting expectations of different community groups, says that Pima's biggest challenge "is selling the idea of what a community college is to a lot of different groups. Everybody wants to make us fit a mold, to type us as a vocational-technical institute, or as a second-rate college, or as a haven for hippies and militants. We've been brash and innovative, and that disturbs a lot of people. It invites repression. How do you break down fear and apprehension in a community? We're asking a lot of adults to make major changes in their value systems late in life. If we don't have enough imagination and awareness to deal with the consequences of that, we won't make it."

Community pressures have already taken a substantial toll. When Pima's problems began to multiply, the local newspapers and other unhappy groups seized on President Harper's administrative style as the root cause of the college's problems. He was too easy, they said; he lacked toughness and discipline. They indicated that the board of governors had lost confidence in him. Within the college there were complaints of poor communication and organizational inefficiency, and all those problems ultimately landed on Harper's desk. He would not agree to turn the college in a more traditional direction to satisfy his internal and external critics. Under his leadership, he said, Pima would be a college that serves students first, that equalizes and preserves cultures, that makes administrators and maintenance men part of the same team. The five voting members of the board of governors, meeting privately without the four nonvoting members, apparently decided that they wanted a change. They did not ask publicly for Harper's resignation, but they got it. In November of 1971 he announced his resignation and—in spite of massive protests by students and faculty —left Pima College in June 1972.

Aside from community pressures, Pima faces some other familiar restraints, chief among them being growth and finances. Its physical plant was planned to accommodate six thousand students, and almost that many are already enrolled, with no leveling off expected. Ironically, the more successful Pima is, the more students it is likely to attract—and the more difficult it will be to meet their needs in the flexible and inventive ways that now distinguish the college. As for finances, they are a headache for every college. In Pima's case, money worries are compounded by the awareness that those who supply the funds—county and state officials and ultimately taxpayers—rarely show generosity to institutions that seem to be marching to the beat of a different drummer. "Educational institutions can't be lasting agents of social change," a Pima administrator observes. "The larger society militates against it. They just cut the budget, and then you're forced to make some choices. So what you end up with is an internal struggle. It can come down to something like Papago and Swahili versus air conditioning. Those faculty members may like one another personally, but they can end up fighting over a budget crisis imposed from the outside."

For all its success in holding its Noah's Ark college together so far, the Pima family is affected by the accumulating weight of its external and internal pressures. The school's total commitment to pluralism will be more and more difficult to maintain with rapid and continuing growth. "It's working now," says one faculty member; "but when we get larger, the easy thing to do will be to become just like any other college." There has been no organized effort at racial separation thus far, but a certain amount of that is inevitable. "And when that happens," said another teacher, "a lot of people are going to hit the panic button. It takes uncommon sensitivity to stay open and flexible, and I'm not sure we can maintain that much group sensitivity."

Some members of the Pima community say that the preoccupation with pluralism causes problems. "It's very hard to get minority faculty," one man says. "We can't pay enough, and when we pay more for them, we run into flak from all directions. And there are certification limits imposed by the state." Another adds, "Even with all the effort that has been made here, I still see that invisible line between Black and white, between Black and brown, between brown and white."

Pima's goal is to erase lines. It has managed to get this far without using professorial ranks or even titles—"Doctor" and "Mister" are seldom heard; and Kenneth Harper was called Ken, instead of President Harper, by secretaries and security men as well as administrators and teachers. By making an extraordinary effort, the college has erased many of the privileges that customarily accrue to whites simply because they are white. It has also removed the barriers to access, which keep so many young people from a chance to succeed in college, and it has made some noteworthy moves to erase lines of discrimination between generations, sexes, and socioeconomic groups. It has concentrated, perhaps more than any other college in the country, on building diversity and equity into every aspect of its operations.

The pressures and tensions created by such an enterprise

could not be avoided. They could make it into a commonplace college. But an inordinately large number of people at Pima seem determined to make it into something uncommon. Their experiment is transferable to dozens of urban centers throughout the country, and it is hard to see it in action without hoping that it succeeds in Tucson and spreads elsewhere.

Third College

Peter A. Janssen

The 1253-acre campus of the University of California at San Diego perches atop a low, eucalyptus-shaded mesa above La Jolla and the Pacific Ocean. San Diego proper lies ten minutes away, behind some bluffs to the south. Tanned, shirtless, and shoeless students, carrying beach towels, tennis rackets, and even books, wander past wide lawns to classes in cubular, concrete buildings. Just over the crest of the mesa to the east, in a series of one-story wooden buildings, lies the home of UCSD's new Third College. There is no view of the Pacific from Third College windows. Still, it is far from being a depressed area; and for most of its 350 students it holds out, for the first time, the promise of a first-rate education, no matter what side of the hill it is on.

Third College opened in September 1970 with the unabashed purpose of educating minority (Black, Chicano, Indian, and Asian) students and training them for leadership roles in their own communities. In no sense is Third College a breakaway, independent institution like DQU near Davis or an isolated effort at rehabilitation and renewal, like Navajo Community College in Arizona. It operates entirely by the rules; everything—and everyone—at Third College is stamped, certified, and approved by the system.

The state's master plan calls for UCSD to grow to a series of twelve interrelated colleges—and 27,500 students—by 1995. Today it consists of three colleges and 5700 students. Tuition (UC calls it "fees") is $212 a quarter for state residents, $712 for non-residents. Room and board come to another $1200 a year. UCSD has no sororities or fraternities, no privately owned residence halls, no intercollegiate football. Most students come from the San Diego and Los Angeles area. They lead a relaxed life, although academic standards are high.

UCSD's first college, Revelle, opened for undergraduates in 1964, with a strong emphasis on science. The second, Muir, opened in 1968, with an emphasis on the humanities. Third College came two years later. It has no other name. The Black and Chicano student organizations on campus asked that it be named Lumumba-Zapata College, but that blew some very important minds in conservative La Jolla–San Diego, and the descriptive Third College seemed an acceptable interim substitute to all parties involved.

New UCSD students apply to any of the three colleges. A student affiliated with one college can take courses, and even a major, in another, although the general idea is to make both an academic and a social home base in one. Faculty members have a joint affiliation, first with their own university-wide departments (there is one chemistry department, for example, in the entire university, serving students in all three colleges) and then with one of the colleges. They are expected to take part in the life of the particular college, to share its goals, and counsel its students.

Third College itself grew out of pressure from Black and Chicano students in the late 1960s. In March 1969 the Black Student Union and the Mexican-American Youth Alliance published an eight-page pamphlet in which they demanded that the university's third college concentrate on third-world students and problems:

> *Having been admitted to the university, some of us thought we had crashed through the barriers of racism and economic oppression. Instead, we found that we were accidentally the chosen ones, the privileged few who, according to the powers that be, are the exceptions that challenge the rule—the existence of white racism. . . .*
>
> *At the University of California, San Diego, we will no longer insure the undisturbed existence of a false institution which consistently fails to respond to the needs of our people. . . . We demand that the Third College be de-*

*voted to relevant education for minority youth and to the
study of the contemporary social problems of all people.*

In the atmosphere of the King and Kennedy assassinations
and with the help of liberal faculty and administrators, the university agreed to create Third College. A student-faculty search
committee selected Joseph W. Watson, an assistant professor of
chemistry and the first Black faculty member on campus when he
arrived in 1966, as its provost. Watson has a B.A. from CCNY and
a Ph.D. from UCLA; he was faculty advisor to the Black Student
Union at UCSD. The university administration approved the
selection.

Third College got a $170,000 grant from the Ford Founda-
tion to develop a curriculum and recruit faculty. In the summer of
1970 Watson worked with a group of twenty students and some
faculty members to draw up Third College courses, orientation programs, and even dormitory rules.

The college opened in fall quarter 1970 with 169 students
and 19 faculty members. It had 117 freshmen, 29 sophomores, 16
juniors, and 7 seniors; 140 were students who had not been on the
campus before, 29 transferred from Revelle and Muir. About 35
percent of the students were Black, 35 percent Chicanos, and 30
percent a mixed bag of whites with a few Indians and Asians. About
90 percent of the students needed financial help. Sixty students were
admitted under the university's 4 percent quota for students whose
high school grades meet the usual requirements but who have not
taken the specific subjects for regular admission. Nine of the faculty
members were new to the campus; four transferred from Revelle
and Muir; and six more were borrowed from Revelle and Muir to
fill out the new college staff.

Third College drew up a core curriculum of four parts: (1)
science and technology, to "give students insight into the nature of
science and its relevance to their lives," with an emphasis on premedical and health sciences; (2) urban and rural development; (3)
third-world studies, covering non-Western cultures and nations;
(4) communications—basic communications skills, including speaking, reading, and writing.

In addition to its emphasis on minority and third-world problems, Third College differs from Revelle and Muir by concentrating on contemporary social problems. A Third College chemistry major, for example, studies the chemistry of environmental pollution; a premedical student spends time in community health centers. Third College students, like other UCSD students, are not restricted to courses in their own college, and about one fourth take courses in Revelle or Muir. Third College does not give a graduate degree.

In its first year Third College ran into more than its share of public criticism. One state assemblyman charged that "Third College is a racist and sandbox affair." The *National Review* warned that it was forcing the university to lower its standards; the syndicated Evans-Novak Report called it "a Frankenstein monster that may devour" the rest of the campus. The *Los Angeles Times* carried a critical letter from Jack D. Douglas, a UCSD associate professor of sociology, under the headline "San Diego Third College Was Doomed to Failure." Douglas wrote that the college was "trying to foist a revolutionary program off on its students" and that the faculty for this "junior college program" did not meet "the standards for university faculty." Ten days later Watson replied, in the same space, that Douglas's charges had "no basis in fact" and that Douglas's "description of the faculty is absolutely not true and Douglas has no evidence for it." Watson said that the Third College faculty is appointed in the same manner as all other UCSD faculty—by their campus-wide departments, by a campus-wide faculty review committee, by the graduate dean and the chancellor, and finally by the UC Board of Regents. The criticism has since died down.

Third College is more innovative than the other colleges at UCSD, particularly in student and faculty participation in college affairs. According to Provost Watson, "We do everything we can to get students involved in the affairs of the college and in the appointment of faculty. [Students review prospective faculty members and make recommendations to Watson. They have approved all those who have been appointed.] If you expect them to participate in society, you have to let them do that at college. It compels us to encourage student participation."

Two faculty members, elected by Third College faculty, and three students, elected by Third College students, meet regularly with Watson as an informal board of directors of the college. This is a real advantage," Watson says. "It brings students into the affairs of the college and provides a mechanism for them to be represented. It also provides the mechanics for keeping me in continual contact with the faculty and students."

Watson worries about the pressures that high-powered campus life puts on Third College students. "If you have a college of minority students, you've got to spend a lot of time giving them things they didn't have in high school," he says. "But they also have to enjoy themselves and behave like young people. We can't put too much pressure on them."

A natural politician, he is trying to organize Third College faculty so that they can carry the college's philosophy into their departments and other colleges when they teach there. "It's important for us to have a coherent policy across the departments," Watson says. "It's much better to present a unified face to all the departments on campus. We also have made a decision that we don't want part-time faculty. We want to have a permanent influence. We want people to study and work here full time." He also wants Third College graduates to be able to make decisions that affect their communities. "One thing we know," he said, "is that society will have to develop new sources of power. We've got to get minorities in decision making. In other areas we've got to get minorities to influence how money is used by banks. There's a lot to do."

The largest problem at Third College, of course, is money. Money is needed for financial support for students, for special tutoring and counseling programs, and for recruiting minority faculty. "Many people feel that since we're a minority college they shouldn't give to us," Watson says. "They say the students here haven't graduated from high school with the same preparation as middle-class whites and they don't belong on a UC campus. We hope we can disprove that."

In his office during the day, Watson had worn a conservative business suit. That night, at Third College's registration assembly for the new fall quarter, he sauntered in wearing a dashiki, the academic Daddy Cool. "What we're trying to do," Watson told the students, "is to emphasize ethnic studies. We study world civilization here—but on an inclusive basis. We include everyone. And the major objective of Third College is to prepare a greater number of doctors and dentists and people who can determine their own lives." The kids cheered.

Watson was followed by Pascual Martinez, the college's director of students, who reminded the students that his office operated a remedial study center. "We're here only to help you," he said. "If the Dean's Office doesn't serve the students, then you should kick him out—and I mean that." The kids sat silent, not knowing what to do.

Later, sipping a Coke on the stairs outside, Martinez said he was worried that Third College is attracting too many white students. (The first year about 30 percent of the students were not Blacks or Chicanos; in 1971 the figure was 40 percent, and most of the 40 percent were white.)

> *What's happening is that we go out and talk up Third College and we're getting whites. They really dig participation. Blacks and Chicanos are not used to that sort of thing. But it's the whites who've been in student government in high school. Student government may be just a token, but at least it's some kind of participation. The whites see us as something new, more flexible, more emphasis on the interdisciplinary thing, we have more participation. Here we say that you can build your own curriculum and we mean it; we say that you can have a say in choosing the faculty, and we mean it. The white kids like that, and they keep coming.*

> *We have to actively seek out minorities, people with low income. We are looking for students with two characteristics—they're a minority and they need financial aid. We also seek out poor white kids, but they're very difficult to identify because they don't want to be identified.*

> *Our main problem last year was paranoia in the outside county. We were labeled immediately as a habitat of radical revolutionaries out to destroy society. A very small*

group of university professors was alarmed over the fact that we brought in "unqualified" students. Now that's diminishing.

We are willing to take risks. We find students who were really wiped out by their elementary and secondary schools. We take the throw-outs, the rejects. We fail sometimes. But we keep fighting the assumption that if a kid is not learning, the problem is with him and not with us.

Last year we had more flunk-outs than we wanted. This year we need to give them more tutoring. We've set up an academic committee of faculty, counselors, and students. We'll meet on the second and sixth weeks of the quarter to identify students with problems and try to help them before it's too late.

Carlos Blanco, a professor of literature in the Chicano studies program, says that Third College needs "a lot more money for tutorial programs. Students need to pick up skills they don't have so they don't flunk out. We need to let them know what they can do. There's no reason that a Chicano has to be a guitarist. If he wants to be a chemist, he should be a chemist. This university only has one Chicano chemist; maybe fifty students now want to be chemists. But they look at that one and they see that other chemists on the faculty have larger labs, more teaching assistants, they get bigger grants. The other faculty have been here longer. We've got to get money for special summer jobs for our young faculty people so they can stay in the university and get to the top of things themselves."

Arturo Madrid, a thirty-one-year-old assistant professor of literature, says that the Third College program is different from ethnic programs at many other colleges. "Most schools tell the students to go out into the community. Our idea is to get the kids here in the university, keep them here until they graduate and can really help do things back in their communities; then they can get out."

Gracia Molina de Pick, who coordinates Chicano studies at Third College (where her son is a student), adds that "the biggest problem is that students all need financial aid. They don't have money to live on campus, and they don't have money for cars to get to the campus." She also worries that Chicanos are losing touch with their culture—and even with the Spanish language. This year she is starting a Spanish course for Chicanos.

Ultimately, of course, much of the success of Third College depends on its students. Linda Clark is a white sophomore from San Jose. "I could have gone to San Jose State and saved $1500 in room and board," she says, "but I was excited by what was happening here. The strongest part of this college is that people are working together. For me, there's a feeling that I'm building something. I still don't know what I will do, but I'm getting my head together now. A good point here is community involvement. I'm on the community-relations committee. That's three students and three faculty who go out and talk to service clubs, Kiwanis, high school counselors. We do the 'You too can go to college' type of thing. Last year a lot of people were ignorant of what was going on here and they would parrot what critics said. But on the campus itself, people realize that we have a definite purpose."

Ray Goldstein is a twenty-four-year-old Chicano who spent two years in the army and is transferring into Third College as a senior from San Diego State. He is from Logan Heights in San Diego and came to Third College "because we need more expertise to compete with the Anglo. I want to be an accountant; and here, for the first time, I think I can find out what an education can do. I can get the answers I need better here than at San Diego State."

José Lopez is a sophomore from a small town with a 90 percent Chicano population, "but all the real high-priority jobs, the city manager, the doctors, the lawyers, they were white. This is the kind of problem I want to do something about, this whole thing about going back to the community." The promise, even on the less favored side of the mesa, is still there.

Commentary: Minority Colleges as Outposts of Institutional Redirection

Elias Blake, Jr.

The six minority colleges discussed in this chapter are almost at the other end of a continuum from conventional organized higher education. They represent an open attack on the traditional elitist approach to higher education. In addition, they use minority cultural traditions as a major educational theme. These things are both their promise and peril.

The characteristics of these schools are listed below and discussed. Taken together, these characteristic themes or principles are innovative in the most direct way. These characteristics are generally strongest in the private minority schools.

Identity with a Nonwhite Cultural Heritage. These schools in varying degrees view the racial heritage of Blacks, Chicanos, and Native Americans as a positive force around which instruction can be developed. In the more complex schools, such as Third College (with 40 percent whites, 30 percent Blacks, and 30 percent Mexican-Americans and other minorities) and Pima College (with 70 percent Anglo and 30 percent distributed among Mexican-Americans, Blacks, Native Americans, and other minorities), a number of these heritages are highlighted. In the schools with a single dominant racial group, such as Malcolm-King Harlem College, Nairobi College, Navajo Community College, that group's heritage is a focal point. DQU was founded by Indians and Chicanos in a cooperative venture.

In identifying strongly with a racial heritage, these schools seek alternatives to a white heritage. In place of a cultural tradition shaped by white supremacy, there is a search for alternate values and principles that are not *in practice* abusive to nonwhites and that do not assume the worthlessness of nonwhite history and traditions. At the same time, there is no effort made to argue white inferiority or nonwhite superiority or to practice racial exclusion.

Whites were involved in the founding and development of the single-minority institutions such as Nairobi, Malcolm-King, and Navajo Community College. At Navajo College, the dean of instruction is named Abromowitz. Of course, Pima College and the Third College are public institutions and cannot discriminate. It is difficult for a member of the majority culture—and, indeed, some minority group members themselves—to be comfortable with the focus on a history, heritage, and tradition outside of the Western tradition as delivered to America through Northern and Western Europe. These Black, Chicano, and Native American groups are in continuing conflict and confrontation with white institutions that subordinate or demean their educational, economic, and political interests. That conflict too often shapes erroneous perceptions of what the posture of minorities is all about in their educational programs.

A key educational tenet is that minority personalities in a white-supremacy environment have been damaged or robbed of their confidence and aspirations and hence their ability to achieve. A positive identity can enable the minority student to go about the practical business of developing skills and knowledge and then to contribute to the unfinished business of the minority groups.

Training for Community Service and Leadership. A prime priority, if not the top priority, of the private schools—Malcolm-King, Nairobi, DQU, and Navajo Community College—is the development of leadership for the respective minority communities. Though the instructional approach to influencing students to be concerned about their communities is not clear, the intent is there. They want their graduates to go on and become leaders and decision makers on behalf of Blacks, Chicanos, and Indians; and they assume that leadership can come even from those who are poorly trained in the precollege years or who show little of the conventional characteristics and qualifications for college. There is an assumption that the students will become the instruments of needed social, economic, and political changes.

The institutions, versus individual faculty members, view themselves as a force for community advancement. There is a simple logic expressed. Our community is not yet being treated with equality and dignity. We are a force to end such treatment both in the classroom and in working directly on the problems flowing from inequality. Our students must have as a high priority serving that community with the skills we can give them. While they and their teachers go about the educational enterprise, they cannot be allowed to ignore the political, economic, and social problems of their community.

The logic is simple. The mechanics of execution are difficult; they require sharply different attitudes about educational institutions. The community is a source of new knowledge for students. For example, former prison inmates can give quite expert knowledge of the criminal justice system, its functions and its impact on minorities; welfare mothers can help case workers become more effective with poor families.

In some of these schools it is clear that such knowledge is legitimated and valued. Where community people are not directly involved in instruction, they are on the policy boards and on advisory groups and are taken seriously.

Completely Open Access in Admissions. Only two schools, Third College and Malcolm-King, have any criteria for admission other than age. Pima College required only the completion of an application, with or without a high school diploma; and many students enrolled at DQU, Navajo Community College, Nairobi, and Pima are not high school graduates. Although Third College must follow the University of California's admissions criteria, it also accepts a number of special-admission students who would not normally get in.

Cost is a critical factor in open access, which is meaningless if costs are too high. Only Pima and Malcolm-King are extremely low cost; hence, financial aid is a critical factor for enrolling students. At Nairobi it costs $600 per year. There are no residential students. At Third College it costs $636 per year for tuition, room, and board; at DQU it costs $60 per three-credit course. Malcolm-King charges only a nominal fee, and Pima costs $60 a semester and is a commuter college.

The emphasis is on performance in a supportive environment that excludes no one until he has been given a chance to see what he can do. Clearly, conventional indices such as tests are not used except for diagnosis. These schools are unconcerned about "the lowering of standards," which is a catchword for exclusive admissions. Third College may have the most difficult problems maintaining flexible admissions standards.

No-Failure Approaches to Recording Performance. The grading systems at these schools do not include a failing grade. At Nairobi no grade below a C is recorded; if a person does not achieve A, B, or C, he gets nothing on his record and can repeat the course as many times as it takes to pass. At Navajo Community College the system includes Honors, Pass, Deferred, No Credit, and Audit; there is a specific notation that No Credit is *not* a failure grade. At Pima a student can contract for an A or a B or a C grade based on his selection of materials in a course; there are no failure grades. DQU uses a Pass and Superior designation for grades.

The focus in learning, then, is not on avoiding failure *grades* but on acquiring knowledge and skills. With these grading systems the motivational approaches of teachers have to be quite different and quite positive. You can only get a student to perform by dealing with what he is to learn, not by threatening him with a permanent stigmatizing mark on his record.

The deeper implication is that a student then must flunk himself out, or more sharply stated, decide that it is pointless to continue. He cannot be cashiered out because of a grade point average. His only recorded average is based on passing grades. These institutions know that nonwhite minorities need more than a single chance to succeed in college. Success in college, when tied to skills and knowledge related to the real world, is vitally important for a Black, a Chicano, or a Native American; his prospects without it are unusually bleak. Maximum opportunities must then be put at his disposal to compensate for previous institutional mistreatment, whether in schools or on reservations or in the labor market or in housing opportunities.

Participatory Relationships Between Students and Faculty. The normal divisions between students and their teachers seem diminished in these institutions. Students participate in curriculum content and organization decisions, and are encouraged to comment on administrative and teacher behavior. Specific provisions are made for students and teachers to discuss institutional issues and problems outside the classroom. The basic attempt is to create a "we-ness," where everyone feels an institutional loyalty.

Prospects for Survival and a Minorities Coalition. Except for the two public schools and possibly Navajo Community College, the prospects are not good for survival. Pima and Third College are public institutions: they will survive whether or not their direction of pluralism and aggressive efforts at being hospitable to multiracial concerns remain the norm. Pima College's first president, the architect of its program and atmosphere, resigned under board pressure. Third College continues to have an uneasy relationship to the Southern California political structure. As size overtakes these schools, no one knows what will happen.

Lack of sound financial base may kill off the other schools. No one of them has a long-term means of financial support. None is enthusiastic about seeking state support as a public institution.

Outside of Pima and Third College, long-term financing is a major question mark. Most have developed with federal funds from Student Special Services of the Office of Education and the Office of Economic Opportunity, which has now been dismantled. In the current federal posture of cutting out social programs, one does not see potentially strong support for the kinds of schools these want to become.

DQU and Navajo Community College hope for a federal subsidy based on their being designated land grant colleges or for special legislation of the kind that supports Howard University. Without some kind of cooperative approach to federal support including Blacks, Chicanos, and Indians, the prospects are not good for such an effort. DQU projects itself as a national Indian Mexican-American University. Federal support will require a national coalition across the minority group communities.

Can these nonwhite minorities deal with that common problem collectively? That is, is the strongest underlying theme in each nonwhite group nationalistic or pluralistic? One can be both nationalistic and pluralistic, but there are some conflicts. Both group nationalism and pluralism imply respect for the special character of peoples who are different. Nationalism in one strain can imply group interests being seen narrowly and in isolation from other group interests. Pluralism implies making a room for all in an aura of mutual respect for differences.

If the need to deal with one's own group issues of cultural, political, and economic development overshadows other pursuits, cooperation is unlikely. In practical, useful political terms the common interests of Blacks, Indians, and Chicanos should be relatively easy to pursue. To this date, however, since Martin Luther King's effort for the Poor Peoples' March in 1968 (which he was planning when murdered), no national collective efforts have emerged. In fact, the various minority groups have regarded one another with suspicion. Blacks perceived Mexican-Americans and other Spanish-speaking groups as hostile toward them unless they are Black Puerto Ricans. Chicanos and Indians see Blacks as doing much better than they in education and visible accomplishments, yet Blacks in their view continue to get more resources.

The effect of the impact of white supremacy and racism on

these mutual perceptions is not shown. The Byzantine way in which minorities come to accept negative attitudes about themselves is undoubtedly involved in the intricate attitudes of nonwhite minority groups toward one another. This writer hopes that this will not long endure. These groups need each other. For example, Blacks alone are projected as 18 percent of 18 year-olds in 1985. With the other groups, as much as 35 percent of the eligible college-going population could be minority. This is a sizeable pressure group for change.

What does all this have to do with minority colleges? Support of institutions is a function of the allocation of resources. The public sector holds the greatest promise and some kind of federal support can have the greatest flexibility. A federal approach to institutional support for minority institutions is most feasible with a collective effort across all the nonwhite minority groups. The characteristics of such support would involve a formula approach for basic operating support and capital outlay.

A rationale is needed for why the federal government should support institutions whose primary though not exclusive role is the education of Blacks, Mexican-Americans, and Indians. Primary role does not mean exclusive role. Others can attend and should attend. The special problems of these groups require an institutional commitment to do whatever is necessary to produce first-rate graduates whatever their entering characteristics based on past treatment in the schools.

One rationale is the special history of these groups in relationship to the *federal* government in its legislative, executive, and judicial branches. If one found that all three branches had, as a matter of the historical record, contributed to the unfair and inequitable treatment of a group in such a way as to force them outside the basic citizenship guarantees of the Constitution, then a special institutional support fund for higher education might be set up to redress the grievance. With Blacks, slavery and postslavery Black codes prevented their exercising basic citizenship rights enjoyed by others. With Indians, treaties of the Indian nations' wars with America and the abrogation of those treaties held them outside the Constitution. Mexican-Americans, due to the expansion of America into Spanish lands, could develop similar grounds. Each group still suffers from the direct results of this special national policy, and it is the duty of the national government to deal with those results.

At this level one is dealing with fundamental national policy toward the education of aggrieved citizens. Without broad cooperation such an effort is doomed to failure. Without some interrelationships between the existing pool of colleges serving Blacks and the other minorities, one cannot make as strong a national case. Existing institutions are always easier to use in developing strategies than plans on the drawing boards for new ones to be built from the ground up. One group of Black Colleges, with North Carolina A & T University as the coordinator, has proposed development of a program to bring in Native Americans. North Carolina Central University, another Black college, has a special effort to recruit Indians to its law school and has graduated the first Indian lawyer in the history of the state. Though traditional Black colleges are not included in this book (and a general discussion of minority education makes no sense without them), they represent a potential focus for cooperation. There is a network of 110 colleges, with 88 four-year schools enrolling about 180,000 students. This network could be of enormous significance to all minorities. The big if is: Are these schools interested in other minorities, and are other minorities interested in them?

Without a sound support base the kinds of private institutions discussed in this section may well become exemplars of what might have been. But then, some observer in 1870 looking at the rudimentary structures of colleges founded for Blacks may have made the same pessimistic observation. Yet today they are producing about 25,000 graduates a year.

Commentary: Postsecondary Education for Latin Americans

Pastora San Juan Cafferty

The development of educational institutions that offer a special education for a specific ethnic or racial group is a significant one in American society. For more than a century, as the nation tenaciously held to the melting-pot theory of immigrant assimilation, the public school became the chief means of educating "good Americans." Such education, it was expected, would produce the ideal homogeneous society, in which all citizens speak good English and affirm the Protestant ethic. America may be a nation of immigrants proud of their cultural roots, but most of these immigrants long ago paid the price of becoming an American: a loss of the native language and a relegation of the native culture to an occasional good meal at an ethnic restaurant. Only after two centuries of striving to become a homogeneous society did the racial strife of the 1960s shock America into realizing that the "melting pot" is at best a myth, at worst a cruel hoax on those racial and ethnic minorities who were not welcomed to assimilate into American society and receive the golden rewards of the promise of economic opportunity.

With the realization of ethnic identity and pride in racial diversity came the challenge to an educational system designed to create the homogeneous society. First the Blacks and then the Spanish-speaking began to demand an educational curriculum relevant to their needs. However, in order to develop such a curriculum, each institution must break free from conventional wisdom and examine itself critically. It must have a sense of realism regarding its assets and limitations and a sensitivity to community concern. It must identify its clientele in the community and ask what the student consumer truly needs for an education.

In the past decade the immediate response to community demands by most educational institutions has often been little more than a knee-jerk reaction. When Blacks effectively pointed out that the traditional curriculum had little to offer them, Black Studies programs were conceived overnight in response to student and community pressure; these programs, however, did little more than offer Black literature and history as a supplement to the traditional courses. Institutions self-righteously responded to the needs of their Black constituency by offering Richard Wright and James Baldwin alongside Henry James and William Faulkner, or by teaching about the exploits of Black cowboys in opening up the American West. For the children of Chicano farm workers, southwestern schools offered courses in the romanticized history of the Spanish-speaking landholders who lived in barrios and brought gracious European manners to the American West. When a frustrated community found these curricular changes irrelevant, many institutions felt vindicated in their original resistance to change and to community control.

However, the design of such a curriculum must address itself to a greater philosophical question that has yet to be answered in this country: Is identification with the ethnic group an asset or a liability to the individual? The answer to this question becomes critical when one asks it of the Spanish-speaking people, who have retained their culture and identity through centuries of isolation in the Southwest and are now articulating an ethnic consciousness in conjunction with a political militancy demanding economic and social acceptance in urban America.

The nine million Spanish-speaking people in America share many of the problems faced by the European immigrants who earlier came to American cities seeking political and economic freedom. Most of them are making a difficult transition from a simple rural life to a complex urban setting. They are torn between the traditional culture of their homeland and the new culture of a highly industrialized society, which has little reverence for tradition. When they arrive to find homes in already crowded American cities, they suffer from poverty, inferior housing, and the other associated social ills that plagued previous immigrants. And, like the previous immigrants, they find that established groups in American society fear strangers and are loath to trust them with political and economic power. They are welcomed only as cheap labor in northern cities and are housed in the slums abandoned by earlier immigrants.

However, the Spanish-speaking peoples have come to America under circumstances that make their experience different from that of previous immigrants. Most important, the proximity of their homeland makes the return home relatively simple, so that the Mexican and the Puerto Rican come to America, ideologically at least, as transients. They come so that they can make enough money to return home to live. It is this factor above all that makes the experience of the Spanish-speaking different from that of any other ethnic group. This proximity, and the resultant continued identification with the homeland, helps explain why the Spanish-speaking have traditonally kept their language and culture and, thus, their distinction as an ethnic group.

This identity with the homeland and plans to return continue even when they migrate to northern cities. Unlike previous waves of immigrants, who crossed the ocean—and later a continent —to reach the mills of the Midwest, the Mexicans and Puerto Ricans did not travel far to find a new home and a new promise. The Mexican crossing took only a few minutes across a dry gully called the Rio Grande; the ease of travel between the United States mainland and the island of Puerto Rico makes the Puerto Rican migration to the urban centers of the East and Midwest similar to the experience of the Mexicans. Thus, it is not irrevocable.

Another important factor making the experience of the Spanish-speaking different from that of the ethnic groups who flocked to American cities earlier is the changed character of cities in the twentieth century. For the most part, the Spanish-speaking have been a part of the rural-to-urban migration that has brought southern Blacks and Appalachian whites to overcrowded American cities since World War II. Unlike the earlier immigrants, the Puerto Ricans and Mexicans came to an urban America which no longer holds the same economic promise even for its own native sons. From countries where race is more a matter of class than of color, they came to cities ripped asunder with racial strife.

Racial myths about the Spanish-speaking have existed ever since United States explorers began to meet the Mexican settlers in the early nineteenth century. Later in that century, when American military forces invaded Cuba and Puero Rico, a benevolent American press enthusiastically supported the education of "our brown brothers" in the ways of participatory democracy. It is difficult to see how the particular mixture—in varying amounts— of the Spanish settler with the Mexican Indian or with the African slave in Cuba and Puerto Rico could constitute a distinct race with genetic differences in attitudes, behavior, and temperament. But, for all practical purposes, the Spanish-speaking immigrants from Latin America have continued to be defined as a distinct "racial minority" in the United States. And, in fact, the Spanish-speaking have tenaciously clung to their language and culture for generations. No other foreign language has been as persistently retained as the

Spanish. Furthermore, a recent survey[1] shows that this is due not to the later Puero Rican and Cuban migrations but rather to the Mexican-Americans in the Southwest, some of whom have lived in the territory since it was annexed over a century ago.

Needless to say, this tendency to cling to the native language and ethnic identity has not been encouraged and perpetuated by an educational system which has traditionally erased differences and thus opened the door to academic opportunity. The American school system has traditionally failed to serve the Spanish-speaking. Their children grow up understanding little about America and less about Puerto Rico or Mexico. They remain strangers in a strange land—ignorant of the political process, confused about alien rules and foreign traditions. Statistics show that in urban school districts as many as 70 percent of these children drop out of high school before graduation. Those that graduate and go on to college are educated to values alien to their community, so that they cannot go home again. They become the businessmen and professionals whose only association with the barrio where they grew up is to ride as dignitaries during Mexican Day parades in El Paso or to serve one evening a month on the boards of settlement houses serving the Puerto Ricans in Spanish Harlem. The ethnic community, then, has traditionally resented higher education because it drives a deep wedge between the student and his community—particularly in poor areas. The student who has "gone on to school" seldom continues to be a member of his community or to show concern for the community's struggle for survival.

To counter such resentment a few colleges, colleges such as DQU and Pima, are not only attempting to provide educational opportunities for those traditionally labeled as "culturally disadvantaged" by our society; they are also educating their students to realize the richness of their own ethnic culture. The student is educated into an ethnic consciousness that further binds him to the barrio. However, the price of ethnic diversity paid by those who identify with their ethnic community has been high. Studies show that Spanish-speaking college graduates today still earn much less than their Anglo counterparts. Rudolfo "Corky" Gonzalez, the

[1] Joshua Freedman (Ed.), *Language and Loyalty in the United States* (The Hague: Mouton and Co., 1966).

Mexican-American prizefighter who has articulated the spirit of the militant La Raza movement, summarizes this conflict of the Spanish-speaking immigrant in his poem of Chicano identity, *I Am Joaquin:* "My fathers have lost the economic battle and won the struggle of cultural survival."[2]

Earlier generations of immigrants found that they could share in the promise of American wealth only if they adopted American ways. The Spanish-speaking have clung to their language and culture and their national identity, partly because they had no choice in their isolation, partly because they always meant to return to their homeland, but also because they chose to keep their national identity. Their children, who are flocking to community colleges that offer an education in their ethnicity, may continue to pay the same price of loss of economic opportunity and deny themselves the ability to choose among levels of ethnic identification. Ethnic institutions, created to serve ethnic communities traditionally neglected by the American school system, face the great danger of becoming not bridges between the community and the majority society but perpetuators of an ethnocentric ghetto mentality which is presently articulated in the rhetoric of ethnicity.

It would be ludicrous to deny that there is a common culture in America—a nation that for two hundred years has self-consciously struggled to create and promulgate an American identity. To deny that this identity exists is to deny that the public schools for over a century successfully educated millions of children who learned correct manners as well as correct English from McGuffey's readers. To declare that this education for life in America is born of an Anglo-Saxon WASP tradition and thus is totally irrelevant to the experience of the Spanish-speaking or the Black is dangerous nonsense. The Englishman who came to America as early as in 1830 found himself in a strange land among an alien people as did the German and the Irishman who followed him at mid-century. Their children, educated to be Americans, mocked the customs of the old country and abandoned the ways of their fathers.

However, this same school system that educated the children of countless immigrants into the ways of economic and social assim-

[2] Santa Barbara: La Causa Publications, 1969, p. 1.

ilation neglected the darker-skinned children of the African slave and the Mexican farm worker. Society had no intention of assimilating these children. The school doors were closed to them, so that they could not enter into the majority society. Today, as these doors are opening, we are learning that the school system did not succeed in creating a homogeneous America. We have come to the realization that the melting pot is a myth and that ethnic communities have—perhaps in spite of themselves—retained their identity.

The ethnic consciousness of the 1960s has contributed to a respect for heterogeneity within the common culture. It is up to the ethnic college to educate a generation of students who will value a heterogeneous society as well as their own ethnicity and will contribute to the understanding of how ethnic differences enrich the American society. These colleges must not fall into the trap of educating students who are able to function only in their own community because their ethnic consciousness is allied to an ethnocentrism that rejects all values alien to the culture of their individual communities. The fact is that the experience of immigration to America created new people different from those who stayed behind. This immigration—whether it was by willful choice or as a slave—is an irrevocable fact for most.

An educational institution providing special education for an individual ethnic or racial group must address itself to several questions: How does the college educate the individual so that he can interpret his community to the majority society and the majority society to his community? How does the college instill ethnic pride without the accompanying cultural alienation? How does the college provide an education which offers the economic and social mobility necessary if the individual is not to be trapped in his own ethnic ghetto? The colleges that address themselves to these questions will bridge the chasm of misunderstanding between the ethnic community and the majority society. Will they at the same time prove to be only transitory devices, which will disappear as their constituency disappears into a truly homogeneous American society? That seems unlikely. Historically, America has remained a nation of ethnic diversity in spite of every attempt by a school system to eradicate ethnicity. The educational institution which acknowledges ethnic plurality should educate individuals able to articulate the reality of ethnic plurality in America and the consequential need for ethnic identity.

Ideally, these institutions will inject into the American educational system a realization of the need to educate for a society which is ethnically diverse; thus, they will continue to function as a choice for those who choose to learn more about their own community culture and as further proof that a diverse society must at last offer an equally diverse educational opportunity.

Commentary: Minority Education and the American Indian

Patricia Locke

The whites, the Blacks, the Asians are all our guests here on this Turtle Island. We must be kind to them and treat them gently and with love because they are like very young children that are just learning how to live. It has taken us since the beginning of time to learn how to live on this island in harmony with the two leggeds, the four leggeds, the winged of the air, the finned of the streams, and the rooted ones. Our guests have been here only a short time. Like all young ones, they push one another, they wet themselves, they spill their food, they pull out the rooted ones, they are too rough with the four leggeds, they haven't learned how to share. But they will grow out of this with our help.

We must teach them. It is our responsibility as hosts on this Turtle Island to help our guests learn.

—Anishnabe belief

Minority education is chimerical. It eludes those who try to define it, shape it, and give it respectability. We have not been totally honest in our purposes and in our efforts to describe those purposes. Some of the attempts at postsecondary education for minorities that have been described in the preceding articles may be precursors of an exciting era—but we are not there yet.

We need to ask ourselves several questions concerning some

common assumptions that have been made in recent years. Only then can we speculate about the really innovative and tentative steps that are being taken in minority education. Only then can we honestly speculate about minority education for the future. Carlos Castenada, in his book *A Separate Reality,* tells us of the Yaqui Indian sorceror Don Juan, who taught him that the task of a human being is to thrust himself into inconceivable new worlds. How can we prepare ourselves for this trajectory if we do not look squarely into the face of what is known as minority education?

Postsecondary education for minority and majority peoples in the United States is education for displaced persons. Our guests on this continent began importing their educational systems some five hundred years ago. That educational system is still a system devised for people who are Christian and who ascribe to the imported values and modes of behavior of European peoples. It is audacious to assume that this kind of majority education based on Judeo-Christian values will work for peoples of different value systems. It is audacious to assume that non-Judeo-Christian peoples should accept it or try to modify themselves to accommodate it.

There may be postsecondary education at Black colleges for Black students taught and administered by Black people, but it is essentially the same kind of educational system that serves the dominant society. There may be postsecondary education at American Indian community colleges for Indian students taught by Indian people; but even though some educational breakthroughs have been made, there is a pervading domination of accreditation by non-Indians, who refuse to allow much variance in the sacrosanct European-imported educational system. And at established and traditional colleges and universities American Indians, Puerto Ricans, Asians, Blacks, and Chicanos are talent-searched, upward-bounded, and special-serviced to learn to internalize and assimilate the "American" values of mercantilism, individualism, and acquisitiveness.

Most minority and nonminority educators have naively accepted these current terminologies without examining the cultural implications. The foundations of minority education are many-faceted and should be based on the uniqueness and particular needs of the specific ethnic or cultural group. Most educators have made the assumption that an umbrella minority curricula with some special services and financial aid would appease the diverse minority groups. American Indians are not satisfied with this homogeneous concept.

Let us examine some of the accepted terminology now in use in minority education programs, terms such as *ethnic,* "Third World," *transethnic, interethnic,* and *innovative.* Most dictionaries define ethnic as meaning "non-Judeo-Christian, or pagan." The term ethnic minority is in common usage relating to minority studies today. If we accept the dictionary definition, then must we confine ethnic minority studies to relate only to those who are Buddhists, Taoists, Muslims, or those American Indians who think of themselves not as Indians but as Arapaho, Dakota, Anishnabe, Dine, or some three hundred other tribal groups who live their diverse religions? What then are the educational options for Christianized Blacks and Chicanos and for other minorities that have accepted the dominant value systems? Perhaps we had better relinquish the word ethnic.

The concept of "Third World" is widely understood by minority students in the large universities on the West Coast, but it is only vaguely understood by the rural Chicano migrant worker or the California Indian living on the remote rancheria. Neither group has a complete understanding of other dark-skinned peoples of the world that are embroiled in complex political and ideological struggles. Instead, their postsecondary educational needs are immediate and are related to survival in the here and now.

Consider the phrases *transethnic studies* and *interethnic studies,* which are cousins to third-world studies in many colleges and universities throughout the country. This hybrid-vigor kind of education is still in the throes of birth. There have been faint stirrings at a few colleges since 1970, but they have been stifled. How often are the respected Puerto Rican, Asian, Chicano, Black, and American Indian community leaders brought into the universities to help develop curricula that will ultimately serve their communities? What efforts are made to help students get acquainted and become friends across cultural and racial lines? Too often there is a scramble for space and money in the minority programs. One suspects that some nonminority administrators fear the coalition of minority students and toss out near-meatless academic and financial bones in order to prevent creative coalitions.

This fear permeates all levels of education. The boundary lines of distrust are carefully delineated in nearly all elementary texts. In history books the Black Ninth and Tenth Cavalries help to "win the West" by fighting "savage" Indians. Black, Chicano, and Indian children read about "coolies" who helped to build the nation's railroads in the effort toward "Manifest Destiny." They read that our nation had to be protected from "treason from within" during World War II, so that it was justified in setting up concentration camps for Japanese citizens and in confiscating their property. Who shall we blame for the stillbirth of transethnic education? When will we really begin to build bridges of understanding across cultures?

What does "innovative" mean in relation to minority post-secondary education? Perhaps a new and different style of education does not need to be developed for those minority people who have been denied access but who aspire to traditional outcomes. Perhaps the need here is only for a wider door and not for inconceivable new worlds of education. Many minority people have truly been culturally assimilated and only want their share of what society has been withholding.

Fundamental institutional changes, then, have not been made. Institutions have only minutely expanded to include Swahili, Lakota, and a handful of courses in linguistics departments. A few minority counselors and tutors have been hired. There has been some frantic activity to hire a few token minority faculty members and to establish minority programs by luring "scholastically qualified" minority students to the campus, so that compliance in affirmative-action programs can be documented. As a result, we have fragmented minority programs across the nation, with our few minority faculty and students fighting lonely battles against majority educational systems.

This view may seem harsh. There are exceptions, although they are still few in number. The University of New Mexico has a fine American Indian law program, Navajo Community College has a program for medicine men as teachers, Highlands University is taking positive steps toward innovative bilingual education for Chicanos, and there are a few more. These innovators who have dared to look in other directions are of the breed that will show us new modes of learning and new combinations of educational bodies. Most notable of all, perhaps, is the creative ferment now apparent in postsecondary education for American Indians: American Indians can truly teach our guests on this continent ways of survival if we are allowed that opportunity. This ferment, which brought about changes in Indian postsecondary education, occurred almost simultaneously in Alaska, Montana, Arizona, California, South Dakota, North Dakota, Wyoming, Oklahoma, New Mexico, Idaho, Minnesota, and Washington, D.C. Small repercussions have awakened tribes in neighboring areas.

In October of 1972 the Planning Resources in Minority Education Program of the Western Interstate Commission for Higher Education, in cooperation with the Education for American Indians Office of the U.S. Office of Education, convened the directors and presidents of the boards of regents of Indian community colleges in order to form a consortium. Two months later, at the Phoenix, Arizona, office of the Navajo Community College, the American Indian Higher Education Consortium was formed. Member institutions are Turtle Mountain Community College on the Turtle Mountain reservation in North Dakota; Standing Rock Community College on the Standing Rock reservation that borders North and South Dakota; Lakota Higher Education Center on the Pine Ridge reservation in South Dakota; Sinte Gleska College on the Rosebud reservation in South Dakota; Haskell Indian Junior College near Lawrence, Kansas; the Institute of American Indian Arts in Santa Fe, New Mexico; the Southwest Indian Polytechnic Institute in Albuquerque, New Mexico; the Navajo Community College on the Navajo reservation in Arizona that also borders three other states; and the Hehaka Sapa College at DQ University near Davis, California. Kuskokwim Community College at Bethel, Alaska, is considering membership. This momentum may soon include the Bannock and Shoshone of the Fort Hall reservation in Idaho, the Arapaho and Shoshone of the Wind River reservation in Wyoming, the Sisseton-Wahepeton in South Dakota, the Northern Cheyenne in Montana, and the Confederated Tribes of the Warm Springs reservation in Oregon.

The consortium schools are unique in that they are governed by American Indian boards of regents, they are served by predominantly American Indian administrators and faculty, and the student bodies are predominantly American Indian. They strive to meet the postsecondary educational needs of the tribal-specific reservation people. They reinforce tribal-specific value systems in their educational modalities. They are thwarted only to the extent that non-Indian accreditation systems enforce non-Indian educational prerequisites upon them. This latter reality may be why the first priority of consortium members is to formulate an accreditation system that will be true Indian education accreditation by peer decision. No doubt there will be violent resistance. Indian people concerned with Indian education for Indians are ready to fight that battle.

There is yet a new battle on the horizon. During the past few years some Indian people have been planning for a National American Indian University and Research Institute. There is a cavernous gap after the two-year Indian community colleges. The tribes, as sovereign nations, have particular educational needs that are not now being met by the hundreds of colleges and universities in the United States. Research for and about Indians is being done to and on Indians—but not by Indians. The many Indian people who are planning tribal higher education have formulated some specific recommendations to present to the tribes: (1) The National American University and Research Institute should be designed by American Indian architects, and it should be located in a sacred place. (2) Undergraduate and graduate curriculum should be designed by Indian educators and respected persons and should include the following subjects: American Indian law and treaty law, linguistics (247 dialects), American Indian education, American Indian psychology and mental health, American Indian medicine, American Indian philosophies, American Indian governmental systems, American Indian history, American Indian public administration, American Indian business administration, American Indian ecological systems, American Indian literature, American Indian art and fine arts, American Indian religions, the American Indian and foreign relations, American Indian sociology, American Indian economics, American Indian agri/aqua culture. (3) The Research Institute will relate to the following issues of American Indian survival: federal and state legislation endangering tribal sovereignty; federal legislation endangering tribal resources, including land and water rights; civil rights legislation and its adverse effect on American Indian people; state, federal, and foundation monies being spent and misspent on American Indian education; Indians in penal institutions; Indians in mental hospitals (there because they are diagnosed by proponents of immature psychological systems); the 4000 to 6000 Indian children in non-Indian foster homes; American Indian biomedical research; economic development for the several hundred reservations, villages, rancherias, and Indian communities; and the treaty responsibilities owed to the tribes by the United States government, its states and its departments, offices, and agencies.

The most probable and serious detriment to the initiation of the National American University and Research Institute could be non-Indian academicians, legislators, special-interest groups such as oil companies and land developers, and most of the American people, who continue to behave as though they are not guests on our continent—our Turtle Island.

We have long suspected that our guests are hungry for our land and for control over our minds. We have been generous with our land. Perhaps our guests will accept the gifts of our cultures. Perhaps our guests will accept the generosity and compassion of our spirit. Perhaps we can walk in beauty together.

🎵 5 🎵

Potpourri

This chapter departs from the usual format in that the institutions described are not geared to serving the needs of a particular student. Instead, they are built on an ethic which says that one institution can serve the needs of many different kinds of students.

It was not possible to incorporate them into any of the preceding chapters, but it seemed important that the reader of this book be exposed to the dynamic nature of these two institutions. They are engaged in the same search for new ways of meeting the needs of the new students, and they have the same excitement as they search for these solutions. Their message is very different, but the challenge is very simlar. We believe that they present an interesting counterpoint to the other institutions.

🎵 Flathead Valley Community College 🎵

Larry Van Dyne

People around Kalispell, Montana, have a suspicion that Larry Blake always keeps a tape measure tucked away on him— just in case he finds another building that might be converted into

177

classrooms. Blake is president of Flathead Valley Community College in Kalispell, a town of 11,000 in a rocky mountain valley in the northwestern part of Montana; and since he came to town to start the college in 1967, he has scrounged about every imaginable site in town to make it part of his campus. The college's art center is in the abandoned Great Northern Railroad depot. The library is shared with the city and county post office, and several classes are held in a nineteenth-century building that once was a junior high school. Other classes are held in the Flathead County maintenance garage, at the fairgrounds, and in junior and senior high schools throughout the county. The college's main building—which houses adminstrative and faculty offices, a student lounge, and several classrooms—is the renovated Elks Temple on Kalispell's Main Street. Blake's office once was the Elks' library, and another office is in a portion of the old stag bar.

Driving around town, Blake points to other places he would like to acquire—the Dodge garage, a mercantile store, and the Eagles Club, a big brick building the lodge put up in the late 1940s with the mistaken expectation that Montana would maintain legalized gambling in private clubs. At the edge of town, by the fairgrounds, he motions toward the rodeo arena: "We could get twelve classrooms under the grandstand if we had to," he says. "I know, I measured!"

Blake's college is about as physically integrated into a community as possible. And being in the thick of things like this is symbolic of his attitude about the mission of community colleges in small-town America. Because these little towns have no specialized educational institutions to carry part of the load, and because the needs of their people are as diverse as anywhere, their colleges must be willing, Blake believes, to offer a range of services that sometimes stretches the imagination and almost always stretches the resources. They must, he thinks, be willing to fill the educational, cultural, social, and recreational gaps left by the community's other institutions, even if that means—as it has at Flathead—teaching everything from tree-falling, horseshoeing, bridge, and small-engine repair to cultural anthropology, calculus, British literature, and genetics, as well as providing exercise classes for senior citizens and running the Head Start program. How Flathead defines and carries out its mission may provide some insights for others who are attempting to develop similarly situated new educational institutions.

Flathead's district—the source of 85 percent of its students— officially encompasses Flathead County, a vast area that stretches 100 miles south from the Canadian border and 100 miles west from Glacier National Park. The county covers just over 5000 square miles, an area slightly bigger than the state of Connecticut. Most of its 39,000 residents live in the four towns and scores of small farms that lie in the valley in the middle of the county. The valley is surrounded by mountains and dotted with lakes that provide magnificent scenery and make hunting, water and snow skiing, fishing, boating, and general tourism major industries. (At the request of the Kalispell Chamber of Commerce the college recently gave gas station attendants, motel operators, and others a course in hospitality.) Logging, wheat, cattle, cherries, and Christmas trees are other major sources of income for the valley's residents. The largest single plant in the valley, however, is the Anaconda Aluminum Company's 1000-employee aluminum reduction plant. The nearest college to Kalispell is the University of Montana at Missoula, 120 miles to the south. Or at least it was until 1967.

For a long time before that, Kalispell's business and civic leaders had talked about the town's need for some sort of college. Kalispell was so far from a college that its high school graduates could not stay home and go on to school. The cultural life of the community left something to be desired, and a college might offer drama and art. A college might attract industries to the area, since they could be sure of securing workers who would be trained for their jobs. A college generally would be a source of community betterment, like an airport or a sewage-treatment plant, something that no self-respecting town should be without.

In 1965, in fact, a group of professional men provided some money to support the scheme of a University of Montana professor who wanted to start a summer college in Kalispell. It was to be a place where local schoolteachers could work on degrees and where high school graduates could get a head start on their freshman year; Glacier College, they called it. But Glacier College soon ran into accreditation problems because it was not a "year-round, degree-granting" institution. Its credits were next to useless. The men who

supported the effort were disappointed; some were even convinced
that the professor, who they thought should have anticipated the
accreditation hurdle, had taken them for a bit of a ride. Whitworth
College in Spokane, Washington, agreed to provide the necessary
accreditation umbrella for a couple of summers, but the project
eventually ended in failure.

One of the supporters of this ill-fated venture was Owen
Sourwine, retired owner of an oil delivery service and a board
member of the First Federal Savings and Loan Association. One
fall after the collapse of Glacier College, Sourwine took his own son
to school at a community college in Oregon; there the concept of
the comprehensive community college was explained to him. He
came away convinced that this was just what Kalispell needed. A
few weeks later he was scheduled to give the program at the noon
luncheon of the Rotary Club, and he chose to talk about the possibility of a community college for the town. Interest was kindled; and
after a long campaign, led by Sourwine and others like him, the
creation of the community college district was brought to a referen-
dum and approved in April 1967. Fifteen percent of the college's
cost would be raised at the local level, with the rest coming from
student fees (25 percent) and state appropriations (60 percent).

One of the first tasks of the new college's popularly elected
trustees was to select a president, and the man they soon settled
on was Blake. He was a Kalispell native who had graduated from
the local high school and then gone on to Montana State. In the
years since, he had worked as an engineering consultant and a community college teacher throughout the West. Just before the
trustees offered him the presidency, he had received a doctorate
from the University of Arizona, where he had studied both engineering and education. The trustees were convinced that Blake, then
thirty-seven, would have a grasp of the politics and moods of his
hometown and a larger perspective on the community college movement in general.

As president of the new college, Blake immediately tried to
get some grasp of what the county's needs were and how they might
be served. He went everywhere, speaking to chambers of commerce,
granges, women's clubs, veteran's groups, and service clubs. He
served on the board of directors of the Kalispell Chamber of

Commerce, lunched at the new Elks Club, and learned about the sources of power in the town. He was a booster of the first order and careful to involve the right groups in establishing and carrying out his programs. If people wanted a course in filling out income tax forms, for instance, he asked the accountants association to suggest a teacher rather than picking one himself and risk alienating someone who had been passed over.

He was quite aware of the general clientele that a community college in a small town should try to serve. There was a large pool of high school graduates who were not strongly motivated enough to go all the way to Missoula but who might continue their education given low-cost schooling within commuting distance. The nearest vocational-technical school also was in Missoula, so that there also was a need for training in those fields nearer home. Flathead developed the usual two-level community college course system —academic transfer courses and occupational courses. Many of the occupational offerings—forestry, surveying, and motel service, to name a few—were directly linked to the specialized local economy. In 1971 there were about 800 full-time students in these courses, about 60 percent in transfer sequence and the remainder in occupational training.

Yet Flathead has special claim to attention as a model of community college education in rural America because of its vast range of activities for adults and its extraordinary array of programs aimed at the needs of every imaginable special-interest group. In a host of part-time and short-term programs, Flathead serves about 700 adult students, including everybody from executives of the aluminum company to the Blackfoot Indians on a reservation just beyond its district. Flathead takes with great seriousness the notion that a community college should be comprehensive, and if some groups or individuals are reluctant to approach the college, the college goes out after them. It will seemingly take on anything. And by 1971 some 8000 people—more than one quarter of everybody in the county over the age of eighteen—had taken some sort of course there. Here are just a few examples of how the college operates:

At the request of a local judge, who needed some way of carrying out his responsibility under Montana law of approving marriages of all persons under the age of nineteen, the college runs a once-a-week, five-session marriage counseling course. The sessions include counseling by a lawyer, doctor, minister, banker, and psychologist, who on more than one occasion have convinced adolescents to postpone their weddings.

The college's community-service branch runs night courses for adults on such subjects as income tax, bridge, modern mathematics for parents, square dancing, body conditioning and auto maintenance for women, rockhounding, sailing, scuba diving, animal packing, and horseshoeing. Some of these courses, which are outside most people's conception of what is proper for a "college," have provoked some criticism from local taxpayers, who consider them frivolous. The college tries to counter these objections by stressing that the courses are completely self-supporting, paid for fully by a small charge on those who take them, and taught almost exclusively by part-time teachers.

The college also runs numerous workshops and training courses requested by local professional associations, unions, and businesses. Most are one-shot affairs to train just enough people to fill the vacant jobs and skill needs of the organizations. Included have been courses on banking (requested by the bankers association), insurance (by local agents), computers for executives (by the Anaconda Aluminum Company), carpentry, plumbing, and ironwork (by the respective unions), legal aspects of surveying (by the surveyors association), and lumber grading (by sawmill owners).

Other groups, less cohesive and more reluctant to seek out help for themselves, have been recruited for a number of programs that increase their chances for employment. The college has run a licensed practical nursing course for middle-aged women seeking a second career or a chance to move out of housework for the first time; a secretarial course, including human-relations training, for women who are unemployed because they have frequent squabbles with fellow employees while at work; and a course for preparing mentally retarded young adults as janitors, motel maids, and greenhouse workers.

Although the two major Indian reservations in its part of the state are outside its district, the college runs a special-services program for about twenty-one full-time Indian students as well as several programs on the reservations. Blake meets occasionally with the tribal councils on both reservations, stressing that the college will do what it can to help but wants to avoid imposing its own programs. In 1970 the college ran a law-enforcement course for the Blackfeet to assist them in policing the reservation.

Often the college moves beyond "courses" to provide a myriad of other services that put Kalispell in closer touch with the cosmopolitan world beyond its corner of Montana. In 1970 it installed special equipment at the summit of a nearby ski slope, so that townspeople could pick up educational television. During 1969 and 1970 the college's drama department offered 185 performances —176 of them sellouts—of everything from *The Glass Menagerie* to *You're a Good Man, Charlie Brown*.

Yet if Flathead gives Kalispell anything it wants, it occasionally provides something it does not. In 1969 the college hired a basketball coach from Denver, who promptly proceeded to recruit what must have been one of the winningest (24–3) and most controversial basketball teams in the state's history. Conservative Montanans did not take kindly to the fact that five of the team's members—including four starters—were Blacks. Some of the Black students had never seen anything like Kalispell—never been on a horse, for instance. But for that matter some of Kalispell's residents had never seen a Black person either. Their reaction, as one of the town's civic leaders puts it, was "less than charitable." The local newspaper began getting letters suggesting that the college would do better to recruit more local talents and not get so many of its players from such far-away places as Toledo, New York, Chicago, and Oakland. The prejudice eventually reached such a level that the trustees called an open meeting to discuss the matter. The episode is partly to blame, it is believed, for the defeat that same year of a proposed increase in the college's local levy. Although the team was a winner on the court, Kalispell apparently was not quite prepared for such sociological experimentation on the part of its local college. After one season, the coach left town and the sport was dropped.

Although its sensitivity to the wide-ranging desires of its

town are its main claim to attention, Flathead also has made several attempts to break normal instructional patterns and to recruit a faculty whose skills often exceed their formal credentials.

The college has no required courses or distribution requirements, although this freedom has been dampened considerably by the fact that transfer students must be counseled about the expectations of four-year colleges. The grading system gives students the choice of being marked on an A, B, C scale or on pass-fail; in either case no record is kept of courses that are not completed or that a student fails. With the lack of required courses, the college puts heavy stress on counseling, some of it in formal sessions with trained counselors but much of it in highly informal encounters in the hall or after class between students and teachers.

The faculty who teach most academic courses usually hold at least a master's degree and are selected mainly on the basis of their interest in teaching and their breadth of knowledge outside their disciplines. Because of the current market and because the natural beauty of the region makes it an attractive place to live, the college has had little difficulty recruiting. In 1970, for five positions, it received 5000 applications. On the whole, the faculty seem intent on developing unusual teaching methods that emphasize active hands-on experience for students, often through field trips. Just one example: An instructor in cultural anthropology usually splits his class into two groups, each of which creates and buries an ancient or future culture for the other to dig up and interpret.

Although the full-time academic faculty are more or less conventionally credentialed, the college has also utilized large numbers of part-time teachers, many of whom would not be considered qualified for most college faculties. Students teach pottery and photography courses, retired forest technicians teach courses in those fields, and a local lumberjack runs a course in tree-falling and is referred to by his mates in the woods as "professor."

Still, it is Flathead's willingness to stretch the definition of its mission that is the important point to stress. It understands that among the associations, churches, unions, businesses, service clubs, and public agencies of its small town it alone is able to provide many of the services that people need, and it has accepted that role with vigor. Perhaps this sense of itself is best summed up by the veterinarian who is chairman of the board of trustees: "Whatever people want," he says, "we'll give 'em."

Portland Community College

Peter H. Binzen

On a bluff overlooking a rich, agricultural valley in nothern Oregon stands a complex of strikingly modern buildings that might at first glance be mistaken for a shopping center. The complex is actually a community college, but the shopping-center design has been consciously carried out. It is part of a plan to make Portland Community College an "educational shopping center," where student customers can come in and "buy" courses just as grocery shoppers buy soap, spaghetti, or spinach.

"Education," says Amo DeBernardis, president of the college, "is the only business that hides its merchandise." He does not hide the merchandise at Portland Community College. For easy "window shopping" he has provided large picture windows in all classrooms along the multilevel esplanades that run around the buildings and link them together. From the esplanades students can stand outside and view the courses in action before they register. For the footweary there are conveniently placed alcoves, lounges, and refreshment areas. In none of these facilities, nor in parking lots, are shoppers and shopkeepers segregated. Put another way, faculty members get no special dining, lounging, parking, or toilet privileges at Portland Community College.

For students who cannot visit the college before deciding on what courses to take, there is always the catalog. Portland Community College's catalog may not resemble Sears and Roebuck's, but it is unlike most college catalogs. For example, it tells the student interested in mathematics exactly what to expect. The catalog gives examples of problems from various courses. In the basic mathematics course a typical problem, says the catalog, would have the student subtract 857.39 from 946.3. Math I asks students to factor $ax + bx$ and $x^2 - 16$. Math II, the catalog notes, puts this problem: "A firm has an alloy of copper and tin that contains 10 percent tin and an alloy of copper and tin that is 25 percent tin. If the firm wishes to produce two tons copper and tin alloy that is 20 percent tin, how much of the 10 percent alloy must be used?"

If this approach seems unprofessional, Dr. DeBernardis would be the first to say that he *is* unprofessional, or at least anti-professional. But he is not being frivolous in attempting to make his college an educational shopping center. Other community colleges are adopting this concept—although few have carried it as far as Amo DeBernardis at Portland Community College.

Started in 1889 as Portland Adult Vocational School, the community college was formed in 1961 by the Portland Board of Education. In 1965 DeBernardis, an assistant superintendent of schools in Portland, was placed in charge. At the time this was not viewed as an enviable assignment. Robert V. Palmer, now the college's director of personnel services, recalls that in 1964, when he was shifted from the city school system to the college, the superintendent apologized for the assignment and "hoped to God the college would get a few students."

In 1971 the college had about 20,000 students, about 65 per cent of them part time. It has become the largest educational institution in Oregon. And DeBernardis thinks that in the next decade it may touch one in five persons in its 750,000-population service area. Much of the college's rapid growth resulted from its evolution into a regional college. In 1968 it split off from the Portland school board to become an independent college district, serving 1500 square miles in parts of five counties. Its area includes most of Portland, Oregon's largest city, some of Portland's fastest-growing southern suburbs, and a number of isolated rural communities.

Also in 1968 voters in the Metropolitan Area Education District approved a tax base for the college, providing money for operations and construction. Very unusual if not unique, the local funding agreement has provided much of the financing for Portland Community College's swift expansion. The voters, in effect, authorized the college board to levy tax millage that would produce $4,100,000 for operations and building in 1969–1970. And the voters also agreed that in every succeeding year spending could rise by 6 percent. Under this arrangement the college is guaranteed modest but significant annual budgetary increases without being required to go back to the voters every year or so for permission to spend more money. Orderly growth can thus be planned and budgeted. The college gets about half of its money from the state, 30 percent from the local tax, and 20 percent from tuitions. It finished 1970–1971 with a $1,000,000 surplus in its $17,000,000 budget.

With funding arranged, DeBernardis has been able to devote most of his time to what he thinks is most important: meeting the needs of individual students. Portland has no admissions requirements of any kind. "We accept a guy for what he is," said De-Bernardis, whom everybody calls "D." "Just because he hasn't been to school doesn't mean he hasn't gotten an education. If he can pick a lock, lead a gang, wire a car, or do other things not socially acceptable, he has an education, and we accept that and try to build on it."

The student body includes illiterates, migrant bean pickers, high school students, octogenarians. Twelve hundred Blacks and Chicanos are enrolled, but there are no special programs for minorities because DeBernardis does not believe in such groupings. Skills centers and tutoring are regular parts of the college programs. (Ironically, more white students than Black students attend the college's center in Portland's largest Negro section.)

When a dozen women expressed a wish to study French before visiting France, the college set up a course for them in a private home. It rented swimming pools to provide kayak training for 250. At forty sites, including hospitals, homes, and jails, it tutored illiterates. To reach the bean and berry pickers, large trailers converted into mobile classrooms visit migrant workers' camps. There they teach basic English, show workers how to fill out a driver's license application form, and provide other simple but essential bits of information. "We don't draw distinctions between what is respectable and what isn't," DeBernardis says. "If people want something, we give it to them." Because Oregonians are out-doorsmen, courses in scuba diving, outboard motor repair, camping, and golf are popular.

What does irk DeBernardis is that not he but University of Oregon administrators seem to decide who will teach some of these courses. The university will recognize for transferable credit only those community college courses taught by faculty members with master's degrees in their subject area. For example, a course in golfing taught by a professional golfer at Portland Community College must be a noncredit course because the golfer lacks a master's degree. The credit course is taught by a couple of physical education instructors with master's degrees. To DeBernardis this makes no sense, but there is nothing he can do about it.

There is something, however, that he can do about faculty members with graduate degrees who deem themselves superior to those without. DeBernardis has dealt with the problem in several ways. There are no professorial ranks. Every faculty member is listed as an instructor. The college ignores its faculty's vital educational statistics. Normally, one seeking to find out which professors at a college hold Ph.D.s and which hold only bachelor's or no degrees at all will find this information in the college catalog. Not so in Portland's catalog. It lists all members of the administration and faculty but omits their degrees. Thus, Amo DeBernardis, who earned a doctorate in education at the University of Oregon in 1951, is listed merely as president, followed by "Donald Defler, Biology," and "James L. Delury, Business Education."

Virtually all of those instructors without degrees teach vocational-technical courses. To keep the vocational-technical section from being stigmatized, DeBernardis integrated its shops and other facilities in buildings with college-transfer courses. There are no separate academic and vocational-technical centers. And the courses themselves are mingled in six divisions. Thus, "business technology" courses join with social science courses in one division, while "engineering technology" joins physical science and mathematics in another. (About 60 percent of the students are in career programs and 40 percent in transfer progams.)

The work load is standard for all instructors. They are required to be at the college—either teaching, preparing to teach, counseling, or being otherwise occupied in their offices—thirty-five hours a week. Some instructors resent being treated, as one said, "like common laborers." But the grumbling has never amounted to much, in part because of the tremendous oversupply of teachers. (In 1970 Portland received 5000 applications for thirty new positions. More than five hundred of the applicants had Ph.D.s.)

Counseling is an important part of each instructor's job. Not only are all faculty members assigned "advisees" but all administrators are, too. Even the president advises students.

Perhaps most important in the college's entire operation is the tone of student-centeredness that DeBernardis has set. He sets this tone by his actions and also by his often quotable comments:

We have nothing innovative; we just treat people like people. The student is the customer. We are the merchandiser.

We innovate the obvious. We know people are different. We try to keep them out of boxes. You put a guy in a box and it's hard to get out.

The most difficult job in education is not teaching kids, it's working with staff. Every time we have a meeting I have to sell an idea.

Who wants a guy with a Ph.D. in auto mechanics? He won't want to fix the car; he'll want to talk about it.

I don't think anybody knows how big, solid, and unmoving the educational establishment is. It's like a balloon. You think you put a dent in it but it comes back.

There is no such thing as mass education; there is education for the masses. Education has to be an individual thing. Mass education ends up mess education.

I told our faculty once, "If these kids aren't right for this school let's shoot 'em because there's no other place for them to go."

DeBernardis is proud of the fact that of some 150,000 students who have taken courses at Portland during his tenure as president not one has been thrown out. There appears to be no questioning the college's appeal to a broad range of blue-collar students. All the student comments that I heard were uniformly favorable. A youth of twenty who had worked as a meatcutter for four years signed up for courses in gourmet cooking, food preparation, and baking. "This is a real together college," he said. "I can spend my time on these courses and these courses only. It gives me a chance to find out whether being a chef is what I really want."

At the existing main campus and another which is planned, DeBernardis intends to refine his shopping-center concept. Among the refinements: year-round registration to permit students to sign up at any time for courses or portions of courses; unitized instruction, permitting students to buy specific parts of courses without taking the entire course. "The idea is that you buy a unit of instruction time any time you want it. You can learn square roots without taking an entire algebra course. You can take a three-week unit on carburetors instead of a full auto mechanics course." DeBernardis admires the computerized airline-reservation system, whereby passengers learn in seconds whether seats are available on specific flights days or weeks ahead. He would like to hire an airline official to set up such a system for Portland's unitized course registration.

DeBernardis's merchandising approach to educational innovation and his view of the faculty's role at the "shopping center" does not appeal to all instructors. The president himself thinks that he has 85 percent of the faculty behind him, but "15 percent want this to be Harvard." There is freedom to teach at Portland Community College. The administration, according to one observer, "has leaned over backward not to be prescriptive." On the other hand, the faculty has very little voice in college decision making. And DeBernardis, in the eyes of some faculty members, does too much for students and too little for instructors. "He has made rules for the faculty in ways that he wouldn't for students," says one of the few Ph.D.s on the faculty. "There is no administrative meddling in the teaching process but no faculty participating in running the college."

What one cannot escape from, in analyzing Portland Community College, is the dominant personality of Amo DeBernardis. In large measure the college as it exists today is his creation. The innovations are his innovations. The backing the college has received from its part of northern Oregon is in the main due to his leadership. "It's obvious how the community views the college, because the guy gets everything he wants," a Portland newspaperman says of DeBernardis. "His secrets are twofold. One, he's a very down-to-earth administrator who communicates with the public. Two, he develops ideas tooled to meet individual and community needs, and has the infectious enthusiasm to put them over."

Portland Community College is, as one instructor observes, "pretty much a one-man show." The accrediting agency that visited the college wondered what would happen to the institution in the post-DeBernardis era. A lot of people on and off campus are also wondering about that.

Commentary: Educational Supermarkets, Flathead and Portland Community Colleges

Harold L. Hodgkinson

One of the most fascinating aspects of contemporary academe is the new, heavily consumer-oriented, somewhat anti-intellectual "shopping centers" in higher education. They do not exist to serve the needs of any special interest group. Exactly to the contrary, they exist to serve every individual in his county or community, whatever his educational needs may be. (In Flathead County, Montana, for example, one out of every four residents of the county has taken a course at the college.) In the true spirit of entrepreneurship that characterizes many of the proprietary institutions in this country, these community colleges are run by strong individuals who leave their marks on their institutions. Unlike most other segments of higher education, these institutions seem uniquely able to avoid the yearnings for higher status that compel most schools to consider moving upward on the educational mobility ladder. Certainly that is not true of the supermarkets we are talking about. They exist entirely to serve the educational needs of those within their community, and for no other reason. They do not intend to become four-year institutions, and they couldn't care less if they give Master's degrees or not. Faculty status is based largely on teaching effectiveness, and teaching effectiveness is determined by how much students learn. They tend to be one-man institutions, and faculty government tends to be fairly weak. But they are exciting places and although they are "nonprofit" (at least in name), they tend to have the hustle and entrepreneurial zeal of a booming real estate

firm or a young electronics corporation on the make. Like the profit-
making activist, they have no interest in failing anybody. They have
therefore given up the cherished role of protector of the meritocracy,
whereby institutions reject people who are unfit for major leadership
positions in our society. By adopting the avowedly egalitarian view
that any person can learn anything if he wants to, the supermarket
institutions provide a vital force in the pluralistic tendencies of
American higher education in the 1970s.

If any institutions outside the business world are skilled in
advertising, promotion, marketing, and production details, it is these
colleges. Every college in the country could learn something from
them about how to create educational needs in people, as well as
how to meet existing needs. Even given the dire predictions about
institutions going out of business these days, it is hard to conceive of
colleges like this shutting down. They have forced themselves on a
bewildered and sometimes uncomprehending citizenry, which now
has discovered that they are indispensable.

As in a cafeteria, no one has to take everything that is
offered. These colleges are moving toward more and more modulari-
zation—if someone wants only a salad, let him have that, even
though he misses the main course. If someone simply wants to study
auto carburetion instead of the entire car, let him take a three-
week unit on carburetion. If he wants to study Hamlet, but isn't
terribly interested in the rest of Shakespeare's plays, then let him
take what he wants and no more.

This sort of thinking is fine, so long as you work on the
assumption that people know what they want educationally. The
person who "knows what he likes" and is only interested in Hamlet
may be so because he has never read any of Shakespeare's other
plays. Allowing him to take only the Shakespeare module that deals
with Hamlet may be to rob him of a very rich experience. The
cafeteria analogy may be quite appropriate here. Cafeterias are fine
for fast, high-volume service of mediocre meals, but very few people
on their night out want to get dressed up and have a truly exceptional dinner at a cafeteria. Quality does count, and the way in
which these institutions respond to the quality question may well
determine what their future will look like. (It may even be possible
that excellence and the cafeteria mentality are not antithetical. I

have been informed that there are several excellent cafeterias near Paris, but if there are any in this country they have eluded my reach.)

For large segments of rural America, too, the argument may be misleading, because educationally speaking, the local community college supermarket is the only restaurant in town. Another strange thing about the supermarkets in education is their lack of braggadocio regarding the pluralism of their student bodies. One finds at these institutions students ranging from high school juniors to octogenerians, from professional painters to itinerant, illiterate laborers. But unlike the average liberal arts college, which brags to the skies about the diversity of its students' backgrounds, these colleges don't seem to think much about it, any more than you would think twice about going into a supermarket and seeing people who dress, and obviously behave, somewhat differently than you do. Perhaps the genius of these colleges, and one of the things that we can learn from them, is that they take pluralism as a given and start from there.

Epilogue

Beyond Access

LAURENCE HALL

*T*he colleges described in this book are designed around the needs of students. Such an approach should not be revolutionary, but it is. For years we have been trying to make students fit colleges, rather than the reverse. When they have not fit, failure has been placed at the feet of the student, not the colleges. Mattie Cook at Malcolm-King Harlem College, Jack D. Forbes at DQU, Ned Hatathli at Navajo Community College, and others have broken that pattern. To them, simply opening doors for the new students is insufficient; instead, the student's needs must be considered in the entire design of the college, and success judged on how well those needs are met. If this is not revolutionary, it is at least rare.

Although we have been relatively successful in providing access to new students, we have been less successful in reaching the goal for which access is only a means—equality of opportunity through postsecondary education. For some educators, access has been the goal. However, many new students regard the kind of access they have been given—access to old educational content and format—as an empty gesture. The high rates of failure and voluntary withdrawal among new students are evidence of this emptiness. Real equality of opportunity, then, demands that we do more than toss new students into revolving open doors. But exactly how do we go beyond access?

The colleges described in this book represent one solution: start new colleges geared to the new students. This solution follows a tradition of problem solving in postsecondary education. For example, part of the justification for starting state college systems was to reduce the demand for more open admissions on private colleges. The community college systems were started partially to take similar pressure off the state systems. It is a solution with some advantages, but with limited potential for real impact unless accompanied by other changes in the postsecondary education system.

On the plus side, there are real advantages when a college starts fresh, with a positive attitude toward the goals of meeting the needs of particular students. As the Commission on Non-Traditional Study has stated, nontraditional education often emerges from an attitude. "It is an attitude that puts the student first and the institution second, concentrates more on the former's need than the latter's convenience, encourages diversity of individual opportunity and deemphasizes time and space or even course requirements in favor of competence and, where applicable, performance." To start with that attitude, to build programs and hire faculty with that in mind, is infinitely easier than trying to change the traditional perspective at an existing institution, with all the grief that accompanies such a move.

Another advantage is a freedom to experiment and fail. This comes easily to a new institution but is difficult for an existing institution. New, small, and less bureaucratic colleges, like Malcolm-King Harlem College, can more easily experiment with new methods, change more easily when a particular method fails, and are less likely to be kept floating by vestigial bureaucratic structures long after their usefulness has been exhausted.

However, there are pitfalls in viewing new institutions as the sole solution. Avoiding these pitfalls presents an interesting set of challenges to postsecondary education. First, how can we avoid the automatic relegation of the new colleges into the slums of higher education? In the social welfare field a long-understood tenet is that "services for poor people are usually poor services." Such could be the fate of colleges that are created to meet the needs of "high-risk" students. Second, one of the advantages of new colleges—their ability to fail—is also one of their pitfalls. The cost of failure is paid most dearly by the student who finds that he cannot obtain a degree or has a discredited degree; and the challenge is to protect the student without stifling the creative energy of the school. These pitfalls are not necessarily insurmountable, and when one looks at the alternative—changing existing institutions—the wiser investment may be in surmounting them. But how?

One of the challenges to preventing the automatic relegation of new colleges into the lower echelons of postsecondary education is confronting the monolithic ranking system that now dominates postsecondary education. It encourages all colleges to strive for the same goals—more Ph.D.s on their faculty, larger libraries and other expensive academic resources, and higher and higher academic qualifications for applicants. All colleges should strive to have the best faculty and learning resources for their students and should seek to recruit the best possible students. But not all curriculum must be taught by Ph.D.s, and not all colleges must start their own libraries. The standards set in each of these areas does not have to be the same for all colleges. However, they are; and we know that Malcolm-King Harlem College, Flathead Community College, Navajo Community College, and Alice Lloyd Community College all feel pressure to bring their institutions in line with these standards and to climb the rungs of the status ladder. This push for conformity is destructive to the kind of innovation and diversity needed today.

This is not an anti-elitist position, as is commonly assumed whenever one challenges the present ranking system. It is a call for educational pluralism. There is a place for the college that wants to emphasize research and scholarly writing, hire academically credentialed faculty, recruit academically superior students, and prepare them for academic pursuits. There is a place for the college that wants to prepare superior graduates for particular professions, trades, and skills and that recruits faculty and students accordingly. There is a place for the college that wants to be the best in educating urban, blue-collar, first-generation college students and that experiments with educational content and faculty to learn how best to do this. It makes no sense to judge these different types of colleges by the same standards and even less sense to judge the latter two types by standards set for the first, as is the case today. Applying one set of standards to all colleges is destructive to the entire system of postsecondary education. If all schools are striving for the same goals, using the same means, they will eventually look like identical fence posts—distinguishable only by size, closeness to students' place of residence, climate, or proximity to ski areas—poor factors of selection.

The negative impact is also seen in terms of support for certain institutions. It is more than a blow to an institution's ego to find that it has not made the top three, ten, one hundred, or even one thousand in someone's ranking of departments or colleges. It may be a blow to its purse and therefore to its potential for improvement or even survival. State legislators know where each institution ranks, and one needs only examine which institutions get the lion's share of public funds and private foundation support to know that the ranking has a snowball effect.

What are the alternatives to the present ranking system? First must come an acceptance of diversity in postsecondary education and the establishment of a variety of standards that recognize this diversity. We need an expanded definition of postsecondary education. One that defines it as more than simple cognitive development. Colleges should be free to set their goals within a broad framework that recognizes the value of cognitive, occupational, *and* affective development. However, there is little evidence that postsecondary education will voluntarily move to establish a diversity of standards. Sadly, failure to do so may have consequences not presently understood.

There is mounting pressure by students, public officials, and the general public to make higher education more relevant to the eventual goal of most students—employment in the work force. The new students who have flooded into colleges over the past ten years have had a very practical approach to education. Learning for the sake of learning is being supplanted in the minds of many students by learning for the sake of *earning*. As more and more job applicants reach the employment market with their B.A.s in hand, additional measures of selection will be needed. As K. Patricia Cross, one of the contributors to this book, has stated, "Perhaps the egalitarian era in higher education will force employers to look more carefully at the skills and interests of candidates and to place less emphasis on educational credentials. When all candidates have college degrees, we will have to look at what they have learned."

Increased attention on the part of employers to actual occupational skills, as opposed to the status of the college, could be just as deadening to the system as what we have now. Looking to General Motors instead of an accreditation commission for endorsement of curriculum is no solution. It is simply the replacement of one monolithic ranking process with another. The losers could be the research-oriented institutions who put emphasis on cognitive development, and their loss would be a high price to pay for an inability to diversify our standards now.

What is needed is a new system of accreditation that maintains high standards of performance but responds to a wider variety of educational goals and does so with increased flexibility, recognizing different types of educational content, teaching-learning formats, and faculty qualifications.

I have some ambivalence about posing the challenges that must be dealt with if we are to overcome the second pitfall, the precariousness of new colleges. The noninstitutionalized college is free to test innovations that would seldom occur to traditional faculty or be risked by traditional colleges. But the cost to the student when a college collapses can be great, and thus the challenge to find some insurance is important. It must be insurance geared to protect the student from unwarranted risk without stultifying the creative process.

First, some examples of the precariousness. At the time the articles in this book were written, DQU was surviving on a limited budget, was trading grazing land to a farmer for food for its students, had a part-time volunteer medical staff, and used part-time teachers who were on salary to other universities. Malcolm-King Harlem College was funded by short-term grants, had little tuition revenue, and depended on a volunteer faculty from nearby colleges. The Rural Family Development project (RFD) was well funded but on a three-year grant from the Office of Education, with no guarantee of continued funding beyond that period.

Obviously, a key to the survival of new colleges is economic stability. Most of the colleges studied by the project staff were funded by a combination of federal and private foundation grants, student fees, and volunteer labor. These funding sources are not reassuring. Federal grants are time-limited, offering no long-range stability, and the 1974 federal budget offers little hope for their continuation. Private foundations have seldom been willing to provide long-range financial security for new colleges. Volunteer labor, like that used in many of these new colleges, can go only so far.

A promising solution on the horizon for new, special-focused colleges is the trend toward channeling public higher-education funds through students rather than through grants to institutions. Except in the first few years of their existence, when they qualify as the educational "glamor stocks," new special-focus colleges have been unable to command an adequate share of direct grants to institutions. Under the new pattern of federal funding, power in the competition for funds will shift somewhat from the institutions which have grantsmanship clout to those which can attract students with federal dollars in their hands. At least for the next few years, it is the new students who will carry the most dollars. This offers hope to the college that has designed an effective education for the new student.

Few colleges can survive on tuition revenue alone, and even fewer can innovate under tightly controlled budgets. Those of us who believe in the value of the new, innovative colleges should be prepared to make a case for continued major investments by public and private sources. I think a case can be made.

We are a society that believes there is always a better way to do something. Experimentation, innovation, and change are accepted and valued. Industry spends vast sums on research and idea development to find better ways to do things. We have also recognized that experimentation is easier in a climate of creativity. In the large, bureaucratic world of postsecondary education, small new colleges devoting all their energies to learning better ways to educate specific students can be the educational laboratories of the future. Many a president of a large college would welcome the opportunity to learn how to provide a more effective educational program for women, minorities, or the large adult population that awaits educational opportunity. But where does he start to experiment with new content and methods in the labyrinth of his institution? Colleges like those described in this book provide a testing ground for new ideas that can be implemented in other settings.

It should be noted that the federal government has recognized the need to formalize its role in relation to innovation in postsecondary education. The National Fund for the Improvement of Postsecondary Education, which was proposed by the present adminstration and approved by Congress in the 1972 Higher Education Act, is one vehicle for consistent investment in the risk ventures of educational innovation. With a ten-million-dollar budget in fiscal year 1973 and fifteen million dollars proposed for the fiscal 1974 budget, the fund can provide major stimulation.

So far, we have discussed the challenges of accreditation and funding. Another challenge for the new college is the transferability of credits earned by students. The student should have some guarantee that the credits earned at a new college will be transferable if he chooses to move to another college, if the new college fails and he is forced to transfer, or if he wishes to pursue further academic training. One solution would be a national credit bank founded on a national charter (like that granted to Howard University). All students attending accredited programs would be able to deposit their credits in the national credit bank. (This would solve a problem not only for students in the new colleges but for those in our mobile society who attend one college for only a short period of time.) Students who do not accumulate enough credits at one institution to meet its standards for graduation could, upon successful completion of an established number of credits from a variety of institutions, receive a degree from the national credit bank.

This Epilogue has been based on an assumption—that the reader has found the new colleges described in this book as engaging as I have found them. They do not fit the usual image of our colleges and universities. They are not steeped in solid, immovable tradition; they lack the smugness that follows years of receiving the praise of proud alumni. Their faculties are often different, their students new to the world of postsecondary education, and they often lack the feeling of stability that a circle of well-built buildings gives a new college. But there is a spirit of search that is contagious and important. Their struggle for solutions, one feels, may have meaning beyond their walls (if they have them).

I have posed three challenges that must be faced if we are to avoid inhibiting the work in which these colleges are engaged: new diversity in accreditation standards, to avoid casting these colleges into the slums of postsecondary education; major, long-term investment by public and private sources in small, innovative, special-focused colleges as laboratory settings; and credit banks that will ensure that successful course work at a new college will always lead toward a degree. There are, of course, other possible solutions as well as other problems in need of solution. I have certainly not dealt with all of them. Just as I hope this book stirs the reader to think more about how to solve the problems of the new student, I hope it will also engage him in the challenge to see that postsecondary education has room for the new college that sits at the periphery of the traditional system and struggles to meet these important challenges.

Index

A